TWO WO[...]

to my Mother

David Daiches was born in Sunderland in 1912, and
his childhood and youth were spent in Edinburgh
where his father, Rabbi Dr Salis Daiches, was a
distinguished member of the Jewish community. These
formative years are finely and affectionately recollected
in his autobiographical memoir from 1956, *Two Worlds*.
Educated at George Watson's, Edinburgh University
and Balliol College, Oxford, with postgraduate degrees
from both Oxford and Cambridge, David Daiches has
become a leading scholar and critic, widely known and
well-loved. *A Third World* (1971), deals with Daiches'
academic years in Britain and North America where
his career embraced a spell as second secretary at the
British Embassy in Washington (1944–6), and teaching
experience at the Universities of Chicago and Cornell
before he returned to Britain in 1951 to take up a post
at Cambridge.

Professor of English at the University of Sussex from
1961 to 1977, David Daiches has travelled widely
and received further honours from the Universities
of Edinburgh, Glasgow, Stirling and the Sorbonne.
With over forty books to his name, he has written on
a host of subjects, from Virginia Woolf to Willa Cather,
from Burns, Scott, Boswell and Stevenson to Milton,
Moses, and the Bible. He has produced distinguished
literary and critical histories and a popular study of Scotch
whisky. Among his most influential works have been *The
Novel and the Modern World* (1939; 1960), *Robert Burns*
(1950; 1966), *The Paradox of Scottish Culture* (1964),
and most recently, *Literature and Gentility in Scotland*
(1982) and *God and the Poets* (1984).

David Daiches

TWO WORLDS
An Edinburgh Jewish Childhood
Foreword by David Daiches

PROMISED LANDS
A Portrait of my Father

CANONGATE
CLASSICS
7

First published in 1956 by Harcourt Brace.
First published in Great Britain in 1957 by
MacMillan & Co Ltd. First published as a
Canongate Classic in 1987; second edition
1997 by Canongate Books 14 High Street
Edinburgh EHI ITE

The publishers gratefully acknowledge general
subsidy from the Scottish Arts Council towards
the Canongate Classics series and a specific
grant towards the publication of this title.

Set in 10pt Plantin by Hewer Text Composition
Services, Edinburgh Printed and bound by
Caledonian, Bishopriggs, Glasgow

British Library Cataloguing in Publication Data
A catalogue record for this volume is available
on request from the British Library.

ISBN 0 86241 704 X

Contents

Two Worlds   1

Promised Lands   157

TWO WORLDS

An Edinburgh Jewish Childhood

Foreword

During the thirty years that have passed since I wrote this book, in a mood of pure self-indulgence, I have been pleasantly surprised to see it taking its place as a piece of sociocultural Scottish history. Looking back now, I can see more clearly than when I was writing it that I was documenting a short-lived period of cultural interchange in the life of Edinburgh that has its counterparts in other cultures and other periods. I have had letters from places as far apart as New York, Cape Town and Hong Kong from people whose recollections of their own childhood among two cultures were similar to my own. Yet there was something very special about the Scottish–Jewish interchange in Edinburgh in the years between the two world wars, that derived from the texture both of Scottish and of Jewish history and more specifically from the educational and cultural scene set by the city of Edinburgh.

One of the reviewers of the first edition of the book remarked that it was clearly a record of happiness in spite of the cultural tensions it documents. That is on the whole true. Further, it is perhaps wrong to talk of cultural tensions, for the two cultures of my childhood did not fight each other but dove-tailed into each other. That is certainly how I saw them. I am always surprised when people misquote the title of the book as 'Between Two Worlds', as the whole point of my story is that I was not *between* two worlds but equally at home in both. That was my good fortune, and I have never ceased to be grateful for it.

David Daiches
Edinburgh, June 1987

A windy Spring day in Edinburgh, with bits of paper blown down the street and two small boys from Sciennes School kicking an empty tin can along the gutter. Across Melville Drive, in the Meadows, workmen are busy building stands and other wooden erections for the Highland Society's annual agricultural show, held in Edinburgh this year, though generally further north. The year is 1919, and I am six and a half years old. I am swinging on the heavy iron gate of our house in Millerfield Place, an exercise which gives me peculiar pleasure because we have only recently moved into the house and this variety of gate, though common in the city, is new to me. I am wearing a pair of dirty navy-blue shorts and a far from fresh brown jersey, and my uncombed hair is blowing about my face. My mother would be shocked indeed if she could see me now, but she is ill in a nursing home in Davidson's Mains (it has the enchanting name of Silverknowe, and I imagine it as a shining castle set beside the sea) and the aunt who has come up from London to look after my brother and sister and myself is out somewhere — with a young man, as my brother Lionel and I knowingly tell each other, though this is mere surmise: we are already precociously aware that my mother's younger sisters should be looking for husbands. As for my father, he is out at a meeting, or working in his study, or busy trying to reconcile some dispute among different factions of his congregation. We children are free to join in the rich street life of the Edinburgh 'keelies'. The noise of the wind and the rattle of the tin can sound like a tocsin of freedom in my ears. There is an air of excitement in the afternoon.

I hear my name called: 'David! Where are you?' Lionel is waving from the bottom of the street. 'Come on and watch the workmen,' he calls. I hang on to the outside of the gate as it swings round and clicks itself shut with the automatic device that still fascinates me, then jump off and run down to meet him. We cross Melville Drive, climb over the iron railings that separate it from the Meadows (there are several open entrances, but we prefer to climb) and find ourselves amid heaps of stacked piles of wood. There are several children swarming around these, and we join them, clambering up and slipping down, chasing each other between the stacks, shouting at the top of our voices. Then one of the workmen, who are busy further down the field, sees us and shouts: 'Hey, get oot o' that!' We shout louder than ever, and the workman makes a threatening gesture. I find myself among a chorus of children chanting: 'Ha, ha, ha, ye canna catch me! Ha, ha, ha, ye canna catch me!' I am not happy about this defiance of the workmen, but I am encouraged by being a member of a group, and chant as loud as anyone. Then a shrill whistle blows, and the cry goes up: 'The parkie! The parkie!' and we all stream off towards the Middle Meadow Walk as the park-keeper, in his official uniform, whistles and waves at us.

Memory blurs the next part of the scene. Was that the afternoon when we landed up in front of the little dairy in Brougham Place and one of the girls went in and bought a ha'penny stick of barley sugar which she licked meanly and aggressively in front of our jealous eyes, ignoring pleas to give everyone a 'sook'? Or did we go in the other direction, past the tennis courts through the narrow ways that lead into George Square and then — but one might go anywhere from there. How well we got to know certain corners of the city! All the streets that bounded the Meadows, of course: the austere flats of Marchmont, the sadly fading gentility of Buccleuch Place, the unpretentious little shops of Lauriston, where the cable cars bumped and clattered their way to Tollcross. And sometimes the more ambitious expeditions to Arthur's Seat, to find tadpoles and sticklebacks in Dunsappie Loch, or southwards through the quiet shaded streets with their genteel detached houses and walled gardens to Blackford Hill, where uniformed nurses walked their gaitered brats and lovers lay behind the whin bushes. We walked, skipped and ran unnoticed distances, often discovering with wonder that we were miles from home and returning breathless to be scolded for being so late and to murmur apologetically that we 'didn't know the time'.

1919 was the timeless year. The dislocation in family life produced by my mother's going to a nursing home, the sense of loss and bewilderment that Lionel and I both felt when we found the normal domestic routine shattered with the departure of the presiding genius of the home, gave way, under the influence of the natural resilience of childhood, to an abandoned exploration of our new freedom. Small as I was, my mother's illness gave me the freedom of the Edinburgh streets, through which I wandered, sometimes alone, often with Lionel, sometimes with a group of 'keelies', utterly insensible of the passing hours. Even on school days I kept this indifference to time. I would dawdle on the way to school, stopping to play with a cat or throw stones for a dog, and find to my astonishment that I was late on arrival. Once I got absorbed in rattling a stick along the railing in a certain rhythm, and followed the streets wherever I could find railings. The thing was never to allow the rhythm to stop for a moment; when there were unavoidable gaps I had to tap the rhythm out on the pavement, stooping, or on a wall if there was one handy. I finally got to school at 10 o'clock — an hour late — and I still remember my bewildered sense of unreality when I found myself walking into a classroom long settled down to its day's work. The teacher was more puzzled than angry, and I was not punished. The incident sticks in my memory as a symbol of a state of mind which I associate entirely and uniquely with that Spring of 1919: the pattern of the world I lived in had temporarily disappeared, routine was succeeded by a feeling of perpetual adventure, and I would discover with amazement that school began at the same hour every morning and that some strange thing the teacher made us do on, say, a Thursday afternoon was really the regular procedure for that day.

We did not go away for our summer holidays that year, because the whole family situation was in a state of confusion. So we stayed at home, and I wandered about the streets and played in the Meadows, absorbing the sights and sounds of an Edinburgh summer so that the Edinburgh of 1919 is still in some ways more vivid to me than the city as it became later. Of course, the city has not essentially changed — it has changed less, I think, than almost any city in Britain — but the rattling cable cars were soon to be replaced by electric trams (which are now, in their turn, giving way to buses), the lamplighter, celebrated by Robert Louis Stevenson, would in a few years be supplanted by an automatic device, and the feel of the city, which in 1919 was still, I think, essentially pre-First World War, was to undergo some subtle changes. But the lamplighter, whom I was to watch with such satisfaction in the early dusk of November and December, I never saw that summer: daylight stretched endlessly into the night, it seemed to me, and even in bed I could hear through my open window the cries of older boys playing cricket in the Meadows and the thud of bat against ball.

A year without time — yet it was only the secular year that lacked this dimension. There was another world, the world of orthodox Jewish ritual, which also claimed me. If I saw little of my father during the day — I could catch a glimpse of him walking down the street in his black coat and silk hat as I was playing cricket, using a school book for a bat and three chalk lines on the wall for wickets — on Friday nights and Saturdays he presided over our world, and there was no shabbiness then, and no running around with 'keelies', and no forgetting of time. Somehow we always managed to be in our best clothes, with our faces washed and our hair slicked down with water, when my father came back from *shul* (synagogue) on a Friday evening (the service was standardised at several hours before sunset during the summer months, though the legal beginning of the Sabbath did not have to be until sunset): and round the candle-lit table, Lionel and I wearing little green skull-caps and my father his accustomed black one, we talked in a politer accent than the one we employed in the streets and discussed quite other matters. And as we sang the familiar *shir ha-ma'aloth* at the beginning of the post-prandial grace, to the plangent minor melody that my father had learned from his father, the Meadows and Marchmont and Arthur's Seat and Blackford Hill were forgotten and we were back in a world which stretched unbroken back through the Middle Ages to ancient Palestine.

But were they really forgotten? The two worlds, in my childhood, were not really separate. The synagogue in Graham Street, to which we walked across the Meadows every Saturday morning, was as much a part of the Edinburgh scene to me as the Royal Infirmary nearby, just as my father, rabbi of the Edinburgh Hebrew Congregation and virtual though not nominal head of Scottish Jewry, was a part of the religious life of Scotland. Indeed, one of my father's great aims in life was to bring the two worlds — the Scottish and the Jewish — into intimate association, to demonstrate, by his way of life and that of his community, that orthodox Jewish communities could thrive in Scotland, true to their own traditions yet at the same time a respected part of the Scottish social and cultural scene. It never occurred to me as a child that this combination was odd or unattainable (still less that it was *comic*, as the idea of Scottish Jewry seems to be to so many of my American friends): I thought of it as part of the nature of things, a natural result of the golden age in which we lived, so utterly different from the dark days of persecution and martyrdom about which we heard a great deal but never in any contemporary context. At school I did not join in the hymns with which the day's proceedings opened (in the elementary school we did not have prayers in hall, as we were to do in the senior school, but sang an opening hymn in class), though I got to know them perfectly well, 'Onward Christian soldiers', 'Once in royal David's city', and many others. I knew, from my tenderest years, that the theology of these hymns was all wrong and that the Jewish religion was of course *right*: but it was one's duty to be tolerant, and one had a friendly pity for one's non-Jewish companions who actually believed in the divinity of Jesus and dirtied their stomachs with *treife* food. As for my teachers and schoolmates, they had the Presbyterian respect for the People of the Book and regarded me with interest and sometimes even with a touch of awe. I used to boast that I was descended from King David of the Bible (which was a family tradition) and this gave me considerable prestige. I once overheard one of my classmates saying to another: 'If Daiches' father had his right, he would be King of the Jews.' Anti-Semitism I never met with at this time, and knew of it only as a phenomenon of the unhappy days of old, about which I read in such Anglo-Jewish story books as *Apples and Honey*.

There were some things, of course, that one did not talk about to one's schoolfellows, because they would never have understood. And, while at home we never called Saturday 'Saturday' but always *shabbos* (the Hebrew for sabbath in the 'Ashkenazi' pronunciation used by most European Jews before the 'Sephardi' pronunciation of the Palestinian Jews came to be associated with the Zionist movement and with modern Hebrew culture), I was always careful to say 'Saturday' at school. Only once do I remember making a mistake in vocabulary, and that was because I did not know that the Hebrew word *yomtov* (festival) was not current English usage. I was taking off my coat in the school cloakroom and chatting to a red-headed boy named Cunningham. It was one of the intermediate days of Passover, when we could go to school though of course we still ate only *Pesachdick* food. Cunningham offered me a sweet — it was a red jujube, as I clearly recall, though the incident happened in 1920 — and, momentarily forgetting that it was Passover and that I could not eat any food that had not been specially prepared under rabbinical auspices, I popped it into my mouth. A second after I had done so, I realised what I had done, and hastily spat it out on to the floor. Cunningham watched in amazement, and I tried to explain: 'It's a Jewish *yomtov*, when we can only eat unleavened bread and specially prepared food that hasn't been near anything leaven.' It was the utterly bewildered look on Cunningham's face that first taught me that *yomtov* was not a regular English word.

This was an exceptional incident, which accounts for its having stuck so clearly in my memory. Normally I had no difficulty at all in living in two worlds at once; both seemed to be satisfactorily related to the physical environment of Edinburgh. The synagogue in Graham Street — it had once been some sort of a chapel and had been made over — was in a decayed but fascinating part of the city; behind it the old streets tumbled down into the Grassmarket and Johnstone Terrace and the southern, precipitous side of Edinburgh Castle, and the approach from the east was by a picturesque narrow lane known as the Vennel, flanked by part of the old city wall. Many years later, when I was a student at Edinburgh University, my father's efforts resulted in the building of a fine new synagogue in a less run-down part of the city, and though like everyone else I hailed the new building with satisfaction, the move was for me a disturbing break with my childhood and coincided (whether by chance or not I am not sure) with a far-reaching revaluation on my part of the relation between the two elements in my background.

But in 1919 I was untroubled by any conflict of beliefs or loyalties. The streets and meadows and hills of Edinburgh represented the timeless world, while my religion, with its fixed times and seasons, its recurring sabbaths and feasts and fasts, each with its own synagogue and domestic ritual, was a world strictly divided into temporal units. On Saturday nights we would watch until three stars appeared in the sky, and then we knew that the sabbath was over — *shabbos* was 'out', as we put it — and one could strike a match or play the piano or revert to any of the usual weekday activities, even if my father, holding a lighted torch of twisted tapers, had not yet formally announced the change with a blessing over a glass of warm milk and a sniff at the silver spice-box whose comforting odour was supposed to console one for the departure of the Princess Sabbath. In summer, no matter how late we stayed up, we were in bed before the dividing line (one could bring *shabbos* in earlier than the legal time of Friday evening, but one could not send it out on Saturday night before the sun had completely set): in winter it came early, and in the short days of December and January there was a whole secular evening to follow, just as the previous evening, candles were lit and the curtains drawn and the world of Jewish time established the moment we got home from school.

In the long summer evenings, when the sabbath seemed to be stretching on for ever, we would go for sedate walks through the more genteel streets to the south, carrying a sort of invisible wall with us as we moved through a working and playing world. It never occurred to me to resent this restriction on my freedom, to feel ill-used because I could not join the wild street play of the children who were often my casual playmates on other days of the week. But I preferred to avoid passing them, and to walk in the quieter ways where they were not likely to be. This was because I would be wearing my best clothes, and I disliked to be seen dressed up by boys who were in their ordinary weekday attire. This matter of clothing was the only thing that I remember disturbing my relations with the non-Jewish world in my childhood, and this was especially so after my mother had come home from the nursing home (I think in the middle or late summer of 1919) and briskly undertook the improvement of our dress. I had no objection to wearing neater and cleaner school clothes, because they were the same kind of clothes that the other boys at school wore, but I did occasionally feel uncomfortable when, dressed in a dark suit on a Saturday or a festival, I passed some of my friends wearing open cricket shirts or jerseys and blazers.

The school I went to — George Watson's Boys' College, which took boys from infancy right up to university entrance — was on the northern side of the Meadows, and the senior boys would use the Meadows as their playground during the lunch interval. In the late 1920s, when I was in the Senior School, I would have to walk through groups of playing classmates on my way home from *shul* on a Jewish festival, for the way to the synagogue from our house ran through the Meadows and by the school, and by some unhappy coincidence the service on Passover or Tabernacles or other of the festivals would conclude just as the lunch interval commenced. My brother and sister and I were, of course, always absent from school on these festivals, and that did not worry us particularly — at least, not until our last years at school, when we were preparing for important competitive examinations, and missing a lesson might be serious. The teachers and the pupils accepted the fact that the Daiches boys were liable to be absent at odd times for religious reasons, and often on my return after such an absence someone would ask: 'Was it a fast or a feast?' That side of it was perfectly all right, and I would enjoy myself explaining to teachers or classmates just what the particular festival was and wherein lay its historic significance (I am talking now of the time when I was fourteen or fifteen). Indeed, I remember several times explaining the difference between the Jewish and Christian religions to my classmates, especially to the son of the Prestonpans minister, with whom I went about a great deal in my last years at school; and I remember lending him, and several of the masters, my pocket edition of Paul Goodman's *History of the Jews*, which I used to carry around with me in order to be able to answer questions and cite facts and figures whenever challenged. But walking through a group of boisterously playing classmates when I was dressed up in my festival clothes I found uncomfortable, particularly since my mother, who had the highest ideals for her children both sartorially and in other respects, insisted that Lionel and I wore suits consisting of black jackets and waistcoats and long striped trousers — a garb unknown among Edinburgh boys, who at that time always wore shorts (and sometimes the kilt) until they were fully grown. This battle of the suits played an important part in my childhood. My mother, who was born and brought up in Liverpool, remembered how gentlemanly little English boys had looked, and with the best of intentions tried to model us on them. Lionel seemed rather to take to this mode of dress (to which, being in the legal profession, he still clings), but I found it embarrassing. In my secret heart I wanted to wear a kilt, but I knew that I had no hereditary right to one, and never breathed a word of my ambition to anybody.

It was in my teens, too, that I established myself in the Scripture class (taught, in the year I am thinking of, by a Classics master) as an authority on the Hebrew text of the Bible, and when we were studying Old Testament history I would lay my Hebrew Bible conspicuously on the desk before me. 'What does the Hebrew say, Daiches?' the teacher would ask when he came to some obscure incident, and sometimes after class the boys would crowd round and ask me for the true meaning of one of the franker sexual references. All this ministered to my pride; and I had been encouraged from my earliest years to be proud of my religion and also of my family background. Whether we were really descended from King David I do not know — the story went that my grandfather's sister lost the only complete copy of the family tree on a journey to Palestine — but I believe we can trace our descent from Rashi, the eleventh-century French Jewish biblical scholar, and my more immediate paternal ancestry is thick with rabbinical scholars and talmudists of considerable eminence. Looking back, I think now that family pride was more important to all of us than more general religious pride; from earliest childhood Lionel and I regarded ourselves as aristocrats. We constructed private myths about our aristocratic Jewish lineage, which gave us immense satisfaction. My mother has recently expressed surprise and doubt at my impression of the intense family pride that surrounded my childhood, but there is no doubt in my mind that both she and my father — consciously or unconsciously — managed at home to suggest that we were a very special family, and what might be considered good

enough for other families (either Jewish or non-Jewish) was
not necessarily good enough for us. We were proud of being
Jewish, of course; but we were far prouder of being called
Daiches.

You would have seen little of this pride, however, if you
had watched us playing in the Edinburgh streets for it was
only at special moments that one recalled the importance
of one's ancestry. Looking back, it seems to me that I must
have largely depended on this family pride to compensate
me for the minor frustrations and irritations which, even
in the most congenial atmosphere, cannot but play some
part in the life of a Jewish boy in a gentile environment.
As I grew older, I began to see important things that I was
missing. That we could take no part in school games or
sports — which were always on Saturdays — Lionel and I
took completely for granted from the beginning, and since
neither of us was particularly interested in formal games or
athletics this did not bother us much. But when I entered the
senior school I discovered that the school literary society
met on Friday nights, and this was one activity where I
would have shone. It was unthinkable, of course, that I
could have attended — the sacredness of Friday night was
absolutely unquestioned in our family — but I used to look
wistfully at the notices announcing the meetings and allowed
myself to wish at least that the meetings might have been
held on another day of the week. My only school activities
outside the classroom were playing the violin in the school
orchestra and attending the meetings of the Field Club on
Tuesday afternoons to listen to lectures, accompanied by
magic lantern slides, on anything from 'Life in Pond and
Stream' to 'A Visit to Paris'. Both of these activities came
very low down in the schoolboy's hierarchy of values.

It was not as though I had Jewish friends to whom I
could turn for real companionship. The Edinburgh Jewish
community was small — about four hundred families —
and there were very few Jewish boys at Watson's. Though
I knew the other Jewish children in the city, and regularly
attended their parties in the winter party season, I was

intimate with none. In some respects I felt more cut off from them than from my Presbyterian classmates and street companions. My father, whose personality and scholarship had made him a public figure in Edinburgh, was known wherever he went: his formal bearing, his small brown beard (which diminished almost to nothing with the years), his dignified black clothes and increasingly solitary silk hat, were recognised everywhere, and people would whisper as he passed: 'That's the Jewish rabbi', or even, 'That's Dr Daiches'. ('Rabbi', incidentally, was often pronounced in Edinburgh as 'Rabbie', the familiar Scots form of 'Robert', and occasionally my father received letters addressed to R.S. — or Robert S. — Daiches, Esq.) Among the Jewish community he was both loved and respected — almost feared at times, perhaps — and the prestige he had won throughout the city, and indeed throughout the country, increased their respect for him enormously. But the result of this was to divide Lionel and myself from my Jewish contemporaries. We were the rabbi's sons; people must watch their step in front of us. This attitude reinforced the natural aloofness of the Daiches family, and the result was that I felt at least as strong a barrier dividing me from the Jewish boys of Edinburgh as from my Christian schoolfellows and playmates.

But the city had no barriers against me; the sights and sounds and smells of Edinburgh crowded in upon my senses day after day and year after year. To this day I cannot hear the whirr of a lawnmower without being taken back at once to a summer afternoon in Millerfield Place — how childhood memories seem to cluster around summer! — with Mr Fyfe (his son is now Lord Chancellor) at the bottom of the street cutting the grass in his front garden and the shouts of boys coming up from the Meadows; nor can I see lilac or laburnum without remembering those quiet Edinburgh streets between Marchmont and Blackford Hill where the heavy blossomed trees leaned over the stone garden walls and the air was hung with a scented quietness and it seemed as though the sun stood still in the sky and time was arrested forever; nor see a horse-drawn cart without hearing again the rattle of early morning milk-traps or the heavy clatter of vans drawing cases of Leitch's lemonade or Dunbar's mineral waters or sacks of coal along the uneven paving of Melville Terrace. A chalk mark in the street brings back the girls playing 'peevers' on the Edinburgh pavements, or skipping to their traditional chants, or counting out for some game in weird rhymes. And the traditional chanting of Hebrew prayers brings back the Meadows and Lauriston Place and the Vennel and the old synagogue in Graham Street (pulled down over twenty years ago) with its mixed congregation of Yiddish-speaking immigrants and native-born Edinburgh Jews with their strong Edinburgh accent even in the singing of Hebrew hymns.

If in the summer I moved between the timeless world of outside play and a religious world of hebdomadal and seasonal ceremony, in the winter the two worlds shifted their relationship somewhat. In the middle or late Autumn the procession of the festivals started: *Rosh Hashanah*, New Year, first, then the crowning solemnity of *Yom Kippur*, the Day of Atonement, and finally the more relaxed Feast of Tabernacles. Thus the religious calendar asserted itself, after a summer with nothing but the weekly sabbath, and with it the claims of the domestic hearth even more than those of the synagogue. The candle-lit table, the family circle round the fire, my mother in her best dress, my father very much the contented family man after the solemnities of the synagogue — this was the Daiches family not only practising its religion in the same way that its ancestors had done for centuries, but also reasserting its own integrity, preening itself, one might almost say, on being itself and not any other family. I don't say that we were wholly conscious of this, and I am sure that my father would have been horrified if anyone had described what was going on in this way, but looking back now I can see so clearly what an important part family pride played in these proceedings. Of course there was more to it than that. We all knew the importance that Judaism attached to family life and happy family observance, and our family were a perfect example of this in many respects; but for the Daiches family these occasions were also demonstrations of the family's self-sufficiency, confirmations of my childhood impression that the outside world, Jewish and Christian, existed as a background to our family, that other Jews were necessary for my father to preach to and for him to help and lead, and non-Jews were there so that Jews should be known by their difference from them and so that my father could show how it was possible for the two worlds to be reconciled. I would look at my father sitting relaxed in his chair by the fire after dinner on a sabbath or festival eve, and glow with a satisfaction that he was there and we were there and that everything was as it was.

Perhaps this is misleading. Have I given the impression that we enjoyed asserting ourselves as a family and cheered each other with a sense of our own importance? That would be quite wrong. It was all unconscious and effortless; we simply took it utterly for granted that we were an aristocratic family. That was something too obvious to mention. Our evenings by the fire after the sabbath or festival dinner were informal and often humorous. Though Lionel and I went over the next day's 'portion of the Law' in the traditional cantillation with our father, we also clowned fairly often, or engaged in mimicry (both of members of the Edinburgh Jewish community and of our own relations), while our parents smiled indulgently. Once, after the *seder* service on Passover, I read to the family and guests a complete and elaborate parody of the Passover *Haggadah*, the order of service for the *seder*; it never occurred to anyone that there was anything sacrilegious about it. Lionel and I from an early age set up as family entertainers (in my early teens I brought out single-handed a monthly magazine called 'The Family Entertainer') and there was often a species of cosy hilarity accompanying our sabbath and festival evenings.

As the days grew shorter and Friday nights came earlier and lasted longer, the impression of the family as asserting its unity and, in a sense, its superiority at the end of the week, thereby setting a seal on the week's activities, would

grow, and the city became an exciting background against
which the cosiness of the domestic interior was highlighted.
It was dark by four in midwinter, and coming home from
school in the December dusk to tea in the dining-room with
the fire blazing and the red silk shade of the low-hanging
chandelier lit up by the bulbs inside, one was conscious
of a theatrical shift in scene, as of a curtain lifted. And
in the streets outside, the little fruitshops and fancy goods
stores and grocers, decorated for the Christmas season, with
mounds of tangerines set in half-globes of silver paper, with
net stockings filled with cheap toys and bells of coloured
paper hanging in the window, would repeat the theme in a
different key: festive windows lit in the darkness to challenge
the December murk. On a clear day the dusk would turn true
violet in colour, and the dark outline of the Castle would
stand out on the horizon in romantic gloom. (Many years
later they took to floodlighting it, which was picturesque but
not the same thing: the gas light in the windows of the little
shops in the back streets, with their tinsel decorations and
cheap Christmas goods, was the most moving illumination
I ever saw in Edinburgh.) We did not observe Christmas,
of course; we kept instead the more or less contemporary
Jewish festival of *Chanukah*; but the Christmas atmosphere
always seemed proper and acceptable, and it never seemed
to me that I was in any way cut off from it in virtue of our
not keeping the actual day. And the coloured *Chanukah*
candles, and my father's tenor voice leading us in the old
hymn of *maoz tsur*, 'Rock of Ages', mingled in my mind
with the illuminated windows, with the silver tangerines
and the boxes of crackers and the loops of tinsel, with
the old Castle looming black in the purple evening and
the sense of the darkening city beyond falling away to the
Firth of Forth. *Chanukah* was Edinburgh in December.

It was strange, I suppose — though it did not seem strange
to me then — this easy blending of Christmas and *Chanukah*,
of Jewish history and Edinburgh atmosphere. *Chanukah*,
the Feast of Lights, commemorates a miracle wrought in
the Temple after the successful revolt by Judas Maccabeus

and his heroic companions against the paganising forces of Antiochus Epiphanes: when I was fifteen I wrote an 'epic poem' on the subject, modelled, in style and verse form, on Scott's *Marmion*. Yet *Chanukah* to us was also the distribution of 'pokes' of sweets to Jewish children after the special service in the Graham Street synagogue, and walking home afterwards in the dark December evening, savouring the atmosphere of Edinburgh at night during the Christmas season. There was, of course, much less commercial ballyhoo about Christmas then than there is now, and besides, Scotland, whose established Presbyterian Church had long minimised celebration of Christmas Day as 'Popish', celebrated the season rather than the day. The real Scottish festival was Hogmanay, New Year's Eve, in which we could participate as a purely secular feast. Jewish New Year was a solemn occasion, the ushering in of the period of penitence which culminated in the Day of Atonement ten days later; the Scottish New Year was an utterly different sort of affair, and though we never celebrated it as a family, we were at liberty to identify ourselves with its celebration by others. I am not sure if I have set out all the factors in their proper logical emphasis. Perhaps there were other reasons for what, in retrospect, I can see as the effortless reconciliation of a very Jewish *Chanukah* feeling with a very Edinburgh feeling of celebration. I doubt if I would even have considered this worth commenting on if I had not been struck with the way in which Jewish parents get fussed about the Christmas problem today. It is a problem that I never remember once being bothered about in my childhood. (But no sooner have I written this than I ask myself whether it is wholly and absolutely true. I seem to remember a faint twinge — of regret? of simple envy? — when the red mail vans came up our street, delivering Christmas presents, and I knew they would not stop at our door.)

All this is the cumulative impression of many years, and takes me far beyond the year 1919, which I began with. It was in the beginning of 1919 that we moved to Edinburgh from Sunderland, where I was born, and that move was the true beginning of my life as I remember it; for I remember my childhood as a developing relation between family tradition and my sense of Edinburgh. Of course there were other important elements, too: there was school, for example, where so much of my weekday life was spent; there were the fishing towns of Fife where, from 1920 on, we went for our annual summer holiday; there was my discovery of poetry and my conviction, formed about the age of thirteen, that I was destined to be a second Shakespeare. These elements have each their own significance, and perhaps in the final summing up some of them will be found to be the most significant of all. But, apart from a few fragmentary recollections of my Sunderland days, my remembered life begins in that timeless Spring of 1919, when I romped through the Edinburgh streets with all my senses wide open and with no preconceptions as to what I should find; and in the background my father, writing in his study, setting out to attend a meeting or conduct a service, and at the weekend gathering his family together to remind it of its identity and its heritage and to fortify its pride.

CHAPTER TWO

In Britain in the 1920s a family did not need to have much of an income in order to employ a maid, and though our family's financial position was always precarious we generally had one. It seems to me that the later maids never had the character or personality of those we had in my earlier childhood. In my seventh year, and at intervals afterwards, my brother and sister and I were left much with maids because of the illness of my mother, and the maid's character therefore mattered a great deal to us. The further back I go, the more satisfactory the maid seems to have been; she was more efficient, more interesting to us children, and stayed for a longer period instead of disappearing without notice after receiving her first month's pay as some of them were to do later. I have a dim memory of a maid we had in Sunderland, called Kate Hoffman, whose German name caused her some embarrassment during the First World War. But the first maid whom I remember clearly is Bella, who was not really our maid but the maid employed by a family with whom we stayed for some weeks on our first arrival in Edinburgh early in 1919. It was at this time that my mother (who had never fully recovered her strength or her spirits after bearing her third child in three years, though she was to make a full recovery later) suffered that 'nervous breakdown', as it was then called, which necessitated her resting for some months at a nursing home, and Bella, robust, energetic, good-humoured and omniscient, was pretty much in charge of us. She left us to ourselves most of the time, but occasionally she would take us on odd and interesting excursions — for example, to watch the buses having their gas bags filled, for this was just after the First War and the petrol shortage had forced the buses of the Scottish Motor Traction Company to use instead of petrol some kind of gas (in the scientific, not the popular American, sense of the word) which was contained in large balloon-like bags that covered the bus roof. Years later I used sometimes to wonder whether I had not dreamt about those heavy S.M.T. buses threading the Edinburgh streets underneath their crazy gas bags; it seemed too fantastic to be true; but in 1944, in London, I saw a private car with a similar contraption, and my memory of 1919 was vindicated.

It seems to me looking back now that those excursions with Bella were often strange and abrupt. I remember finding myself more than once having tea with an unknown family in an unfamiliar house, whither I had been whisked off by Bella to be left there until she had time to call for me. I am not sure to this day who those families were, though they were probably friends of the people with whom we were staying, and I remember how my initial sense of bewilderment at being deposited among strange but kindly faces soon gave way to a pragmatic acceptance of each situation as I found it and a determination to eat as much as I could in an unobtrusive way. I associate these visits with seed-cake, of which I ate large quantities on principle, as it were, without really liking it. Even now, the taste of seed-cake, like Proust's *madeleine*, brings back the smell and clatter of a crowded tea table in a flat in Leith Walk or Spottiswoode with well meaning but to me thoroughly offensive grown-up faces looming through piles of cakes and sandwiches to ask fatuous questions about my personal life. Once there was a young lady at a piano warbling a love song at an enraptured young man, and I delighted all the grown-ups present by saying sententiously (having recently seen or heard the remark somewhere): 'People who write love poems should remember that the only word which rhymes with "Cupid" is "stupid".' This earned for me a reputation for literary precocity which I cheerfully accepted. I needed all the help

I could to stand up to the strangeness of these tea-parties which so suddenly materialised out of nowhere. It seemed to me that there were people who, like the Mad Hatter, the March Hare and the Dormouse, were perpetually having tea, and that other people wandered in and out among the cups and saucers at will.

Soon after, we moved to our own house in Millerfield Place where, after my mother had come back from the nursing home, we had a procession of maids of our own. Training a Scottish maid to work in a rabbinical household was an elaborate business: my mother would have to explain about the different dishes for meat and milk, the impossibility of washing dishes in soap (which contained animal fat), the importance of using different dish-cloths for *milchig* and *fleischig* dishes (blue bordered for the former, red for the latter), the special requirements for sabbaths and festivals. They were always very astonished at first, but soon came to take it all as a matter of course, picking up the appropriate Hebrew or Yiddish terms and pronouncing them with a rich Scots accent. My mother always took a great interest in the maids' personal life, lending them books to read, letting them have an extra afternoon off if there was anything especially interesting on in town, giving them help and advice in their love affairs and other problems. Often they came to us raw and untrained and my mother worked with them and trained them thoroughly in the various arts of household management. To us children a maid was a companion and a source of all kinds of odd information. (Not all of the information was accurate. For years I believed that lunatics were removed to the asylum in a yellow cab with red wheels, because a maid had told me that, as a joke I suppose.) They generally came from neighbouring towns and villages — Bathgate in one case, I remember, and in another Bo'ness — and occasionally one of them took me to her home for tea, an experience looked forward to chiefly for the bus or train ride involved.

One of our most successful maids, who stayed with us

for a long time and only left to get married, was a girl called Dorothy Greenwood, who hailed from Yorkshire. She had an extraordinary gift for story telling, and would tell us macabre tales of haunted castles which occasionally led to my waking screaming in the night. Many years later, when I read Horace Walpole's *Castle of Otranto*, I recognised the *genre* as that to which Dorothy's stories had belonged, though I am sure she had neither read nor heard of Horace Walpole. Other maids were less gifted. We once had an elderly maid called Jane, who had the fascinating habit of muttering to herself, though we could never make out what she said. One day my brother Lionel and I got up very early and crept quietly downstairs to hide behind the dining-room sofa while Jane laid the breakfast, so that we could hear what she was saying to herself. But though we were successful in concealing ourselves and had the satisfaction of seeing her dust the room and set the table oblivious of our watching eyes, we were not able to make out a word of her mutterings. She was a pathetic old soul, and how she landed up as a housemaid at her time of life I don't know. Every year after the First World War it grew increasingly difficult to get a good maid, at least for the wages that we could afford to pay. I remember especially how delinquent many of the later ones were at dusting. My mother would come downstairs and run her finger over the sideboard or the mantel, which was supposed to have been dusted that morning. She would then inspect her finger, find it covered with dust, and exclaim disgustedly. 'Pig!' (But she never said this when the maid was present, being always gentle and courteous with her.) We children would make good-humoured fun of her finger-testing, and to this day it is a joke among us to run a finger over a piece of furniture, examine the finger, and exclaim 'Pig!'

While my mother was well, my father had little contact with the maid. When he was not out at one of his innumerable meetings or at the synagogue he stayed in his study, reading or writing, and his study was a sacrosanct room which no maid entered, except when he was out, to dust it. But the maid had the duty of answering the door, and ushering into the study people who called on my father, who would range from heavily bearded emissaries from rabbinical colleges in Eastern Europe to the Professor of Hebrew or of Logic and Metaphysics at Edinburgh University. Some of the callers knew no English, and curious mutually unintelligible dialogues between maid and visitor would go on at the front door until my father came out to see what was going on or my mother came to the rescue. Sometimes an extremely impressive looking visitor would turn out to be a crook: I remember a venerable looking couple of gentlemen who claimed to be collecting for some European *Yeshivah* (rabbinical college) but whom we later discovered, with the help of the police, to have been collecting only for themselves. My father was continually being visited by collectors, beggars, émigrés, scholars, talmudists, clergymen, distressed persons, eccentrics, fakers, and he was generally able at a glance to distinguish the genuine from the counterfeit — something which I was never able to do, for I found myself nearly always most impressed by the least worthy. I remember once two young men arrived at the house, speaking only Yiddish, and alleged that they had just arrived by cargo-boat at Leith from some Baltic port, and were penniless and starving. My mother made them a huge meal, while my father cannily telephoned the appropriate offices at Leith to find out whether in fact a boat from that Baltic port had arrived that day. He found that none had. It turned out eventually that the men had arrived by train from Newcastle, and that they were making a systematic tour of the Jewish communities of Britain, telling a different hard-luck story at each one and collecting free meals and substantial sums in cash. Such gross abuses were, of course, infrequent; most of the distressed persons who arrived at our house in search of help were in genuine need; but the well-known charitableness of Jewish communities towards needy brethren from any part of the world did encourage the occasional confidence trick.

My mother had to be ready at a moment's notice to

give any one of this miscellaneous collection of visitors a meal. She was not often caught unprepared, but I recall one Wednesday afternoon (early closing day, when the shops shut at one) when she was suddenly called upon to provide a substantial repast for a hungry *meshullach* (emissary from a *Yeshivah*) at the awkward hour of 3.30 p.m. The only food in the house was for the family's dinner that night. I was sent to borrow some eggs from a neighbour and the *meshullach* had to be content with boiled eggs and vast quantities of bread-and-butter, which he ate, it seemed to me, with an almost contemptuous air. On another occasion my mother had just prepared supper for my father and herself and, by some chapter of accidents, had nothing in the way of food left in the house apart from what she had prepared, when a venerable looking gentleman made his way unannounced into the dining-room. My mother, in some embarrassment, explained the circumstances, and apologised for not being able to give him a meal, at which he smiled and sat down at her place and fell to. My mother went into the kitchen and shared the maid's supper.

To the maid, my father was always 'the Master' or 'the Doctor', and was referred to with a certain amount of awe. 'We must have lunch prompt today', my mother would say, 'because the doctor has a meeting at two o'clock.' The maid must have thought of my father as moving in a mysterious multi-lingual world, full of oddly dressed characters and strange and impressive rituals. After the main meal of the day we would say the long Hebrew grace, singing out the beginning and the end of certain paragraphs, and the maid would move around the table collecting the dirty dishes and listening. If my father introduced a new tune, as he would occasionally do, the maid might comment to one of us later in the kitchen: 'Yon was a nice tune the doctor had today.' When we were very young we had no self-consciousness at all in discussing these matters with the maid; but as we grew older we became more reticent.

When my mother was ill, and she had a number of spells of illness, sometimes fairly long, in the 1920s, my father would come into closer contact with the maid. He would have to go into the kitchen sometimes and give orders himself, speaking always in a tone of extreme politeness, and referring to my mother as 'the Mistress'. 'Oh, Mary, the mistress would like you to bring up a cup of tea. Would you please do that?' 'I think we might have dinner now, Mary.' He was not exactly shy of the maid, but he clearly felt that this was a kind of human being of which he had no real knowledge and he spoke to her with a certain caution, as one might speak to an animal of whose disposition one was ignorant. There were sometimes quite long periods when there was no maid, and mother was ill, and my father would wrestle with domestic affairs himself. There was one period when he used to get up early and make porridge while we children helped in various ways (I used to light the fires and clean the shoes), and I have a clear picture of him standing by the stove in his dressing-gown, stirring the porridge while admonishing us to hurry or we should be late for school.

The most serious problem that arose when we had no maid was the lighting of fires and the turning on of the gas on the sabbath, when such activity was forbidden. There was a little grocery shop, Cameron's, round the corner, where we used to get some of our groceries, and they had a messenger boy ('message boy' was the term we used) whom we were sometimes able to get to come in and put a match to the fire or the gas stove. The boy regarded us as quite mad. 'See,' he said to my mother the first time he was asked to come in and light the gas, 'it's quite easy. Ye just turn this wee handle and then pit the light tae the wee holes.' 'I know how to do it,' replied my mother calmly, 'but this is the Jewish sabbath and I may not strike a light.' The boy's jaw dropped, and he looked at her sideways, half scared. But later he came to take it all for granted. Sometimes, when Cameron's boy was not available, my mother would go into the street and ask anyone she could find to come in and light the gas. I remember an occasional bewildered stranger being led into the kitchen to put a match under the soup. When I was a little older I would ask my father what one was supposed to do in a community where everybody was Jewish and there were no *goyim* to light the gas, but I cannot remember ever receiving a satisfactory answer. The logical answer, I suppose, would have been that everybody would have to stay cold, and we had some experience of that state on winter Saturday afternoons when there was no maid and no temporary substitute.

We always had dinner about one o'clock on Saturdays, soon after we came home from *shul*. After dinner my parents would take a nap and we children would be left to read in the dining-room (which was also the living-room). On a winter's day when we had a maid, we would sit round a roaring fire and read, helping ourselves at regular intervals from a large bag of boiled sweets which Mother provided every weekend; they came from Cooper's, the large Edinburgh grocers with branches all over the city, and were technically known as 'Cooper's finest boilings', a description we considered expressive and appropriate. When there was no maid, we would huddle round a small electric radiator which would warm only those parts of the body immediately in front of it. I don't think I have ever been so cold as I have been sitting reading in our unheated house in Edinburgh on a winter Saturday afternoon. On one such afternoon I was reading an account of Scott's final and fatal expedition to the Antarctic, and the coldness of the scene described in the book mingled with the coldness of the room to produce in me the impression that I was slowly freezing to death, and it was a long time before I felt really warm again. The South Pole, Cooper's finest boilings and the coldness of our dining-room are still connected in my imagination.

The electric radiator — which did, I suppose, make some difference, though memory links it only with extreme cold — could be switched on and off on the sabbath, as the electric light also could, in accordance with a decision of my father's which differentiated his position sharply from that of my grandfather, patriarchal rabbi of an orthodox Jewish congregation in Leeds, who would have been shocked if he had known how cavalierly we treated electricity. Gas light or heat, which required the striking of a match, was another matter: that was clearly prohibited. But electricity was a phenomenon unrecognised by the Talmud, and my father felt free to make his own interpretation of the nature of the act of switching on the electric light or heat. He decided that it was not technically 'kindling a fire', which a biblical injunction prohibits in the home on the sabbath.

The coldness of maidless winter Saturdays I took to be a part of the nature of things, and it never occurred to me to complain or rebel, or to feel in any degree sorry for myself. It seems to me now that I accepted a great deal of physical discomfort as a child with extraordinary equanimity: perhaps all children do and always have done. In the winter time the bottoms of my short trousers would rub against the inside of my leg, above the knee, causing a painful irritation that lasted for months, and which sometimes became so acute that walking was most uncomfortable. But I never mentioned this to anybody, and I am sure that my mother never knew anything about it. It was part of winter, like getting up at seven o'clock in an icy cold bedroom and proceeding to have a cold bath (which I had been told was good for the physique). Every winter morning began with that tremendous summoning of the will to enable me to leave the beatific warmth of my bed for the cold linoleum floor of the chill bedroom; time never made it any easier; it was always an act of tremendous resolution, worked up with enormous effort. Yet it never occurred to me that the situation was anything to complain of, and the notion that bedrooms might be heated (except in cases of illness) would have struck me as bizarre in the extreme if I had ever heard of it, which I hadn't. Exercising the will became almost an obsession with me during parts of my childhood. Nobody compelled me to have cold baths on winter mornings — my brother Lionel, though he started when I did, soon gave them up — but I felt that I had to challenge myself to keep on having them without any interruption (except on sabbath mornings, when one never took a bath), and the more I was tempted to skip it for this one morning the more fiercely something inside me compelled me to go through with it.

In spite of these cold occasions, memories of light and warmth and festivity predominate in my recollections of childhood. Jewish family life makes much of the domestic festival, and the lighted candles, the large clean white tablecloth, the abundant food, made every Sabbath and festival eve a celebratory occasion. We would often have visitors, especially on Friday nights, and these visitors might be anybody from internationally famous scholars or diplomats to an itinerant collector for an Eastern European rabbinical seminary. I remember Persian businessmen, American rotarians, Zionist publicists from all parts of the world, a Swedish industrialist, a Palestinian student of veterinary surgery, Congressman Sol Bloom and his daughter on their way back from Switzerland where the Congressman pressed (in vain) the claims of his reformed calendar on the appropriate committee of the League of Nations, and lecturers and preachers galore. Every visitor to Edinburgh who had any Jewish connection at all seemed to land up sooner or later having dinner with us, and the result was that Lionel and Sylvia and I were early accustomed to take completely for granted the presence at a meal of an odd or a distinguished visitor. And in spite of my father's dignity of character and tendency to formality in speech, he was always tolerant of our interruptions, allowing us a remarkably free conversational play among the guests, so that from our tenderest years we would argue cheerfully with world famous philosophers and dispute the confident generalisations of authoritative scholars. Talk was neither rationed nor disciplined in our family: it seems to me that we talked pretty nearly all the time. Lionel and Sylvia and I were always arguing; we would argue with our parents whenever we got the chance; and when there were visitors we took it for granted that we would argue with them. We were thus accustomed from our earliest years to accept lively conversation as a normal part of living, a civilised point of view that far too few people share.

As we grew older, we children would argue about religion with our father, pressing him to defend the value of certain aspects of Jewish ritual or to explain the morality of certain actions of biblical heroes. I remember once being struck by the fact that the phrase 'the fear of Heaven and the fear of sin' occurs in a certain Hebrew prayer, denoting two desirable qualities in the good man, and though the English translation differentiated between the two 'fears' by translating the first as 'fear' and the second as 'dread', the Hebrew word was the same, *yirath*, in each case. I asked my father once at dinner — I think I was twelve years old at the time — whether we were really supposed to adopt the same attitude to God as we were to adopt towards sin, and when he replied that the word had a different sense in each case, I was far from satisfied, and vehemently protested against the misleading of people by such loose diction. On another occasion I objected to the holding up of Abraham's willingness to sacrifice Isaac as something virtuous (this biblical story still horrifies me); it was a revolting thing that Abraham had been asked to do, and the only proper conclusion for him to draw, if he thought that God was in earnest, was that this was not God speaking at all, but some evil spirit. And all three of us children were continually urging our father to preach against specific things we disliked in the behaviour of the Jews of Edinburgh rather than produce grand and eloquent orations about Judaism in general. Not that we disapproved of the grand eloquent orations; we were thrilled by them and proud of our father for being able to produce them; but we were — all three of us, I think — frequently bothered by the problem of the relation of ritual to practical ethics. We would press the claims of moral behaviour over ritual scrupulousness, and would indignantly argue that it was much worse morally to engage in dubious business practices than to fail to go to synagogue regularly. (Fundamentally, I think my father agreed with us on this, and he was much concerned with the honour and civic virtue of the members of the Edinburgh Jewish community; but he considered it a major part of his duty to safeguard the integrity of the Jewish tradition, and ritual observance was of the first importance in keeping that tradition alive and in fostering a Jewish religious consciousness.) We were not, at this stage, in rebellion, nor did we have the slightest sympathy with rebellion or even lax observance in others; we fully accepted orthodoxy and all its implications in daily practice, and we admired our father and were sure that he was always right. But we felt the need to ventilate with him all points that puzzled or annoyed us, and, oddly enough (though not really oddly, if one considers the atmosphere that prevailed in our family), he never took our arguments and objections as signs of backsliding or even of doubt about orthodoxy. Those who do not know what it is to have grown up in a family both highly orthodox and highly critical might find it hard to understand this combination of freedom of discussion with rigidity of behaviour; to me it seems the most natural thing in the world, even now, when am far from my childhood position on these matters. As often as not, my father would listen smilingly to our arguments or expressions of indignation, as though amused at the enthusiasm of youth, and would answer in perfect good humour. As the years went by, we gradually forced from him in argument a fairly complete system of Jewish apologetics, and I am sure that this helped him enormously in lecturing to students (as he often did) and meeting the arguments they presented in discussion after the lecture.

Sometimes he would get into violent arguments with brash young men who heckled him after one of his lectures at the Jewish Literary Society or the University Jewish Society. I remember a Russian student called Krom who took a militant atheist-communist line and had no inhibitions at all about expressing his contempt for religion and for the whole middle-class way of life. Though my father was admirable at expounding lucidly and persuasively his own particular brand of Jewish religious humanism ('I didn't know that Judaism was so utilitarian' was the dry comment of one of his hecklers after he had explained that only with a religious

David Daiches

tradition and in relation to a divinely inspired code of morals could men lead truly full and satisfying lives) he was less good in the quick give-and-take of argument from the floor. He was not a quick thinker, and he did not always see the precise point that was being made. In our own domestic arguments with him we children had often to press him and say: 'Yes, but that's not what I meant. What I meant was . . .' If his thinking was fairly slow, it was deep enough, and once he had thought a point out he could express it with deceptive clarity. Only occasionally, when we pressed him too hard, he would answer shortly that we would understand that when we were older. And he believed that we would. He himself must have had, I feel sure, his own philosophical doubts and objections, and had eventually worked out for himself a philosophy of orthodox Judaism which combined a Kantian ethic with a profound respect for the rabbinical tradition and achievement. I am sure now that he thought that our youthful questions would all eventually be resolved in some such synthesis, and it never seems to have occurred to him that the synthesis between Judaism and modern western thought which he had worked out for himself—with its social implications as to how Jews could live in such a country as Britain at once part of the general community and apart from it — might not serve for another generation, nor did he see what an extraordinary state of unstable equilibrium his own position represented.

My father seemed to take for granted that his own vast knowledge of Hebrew and rabbinics and Jewish religious philosophy would somehow filter down to us without too much active effort on his part. His own strenuous youth, in which he absorbed two different streams of education with a completeness that has always astonished me, was part of a world he had put behind him; he did not seem to expect us to emulate his own extraordinary feats of academic endurance. We belonged to the modern western world which he had trained himself to cope with and to which he had so thoroughly adjusted his own religious position without giving up anything material in Jewish orthodoxy.

Our Jewish knowledge and traditions we would get as a matter of course, because we were Daicheses and his sons; our secular education we must work for. He thus took great interest in our schooling and would talk to us about our progress in Latin and Greek and mathematics, throwing Greek quotations from the *Odyssey* at us to see if we could translate them or asking what proposition in Euclid we were working at. True, he gave us Hebrew lessons, and as far as I can remember I was able to read Hebrew before I could read English (I suspect it was my mother who taught me to read both languages): I cannot recollect a time when the reading of Hebrew did not come automatically to me. But his lessons were unsystematic and sporadic, and were sometimes interrupted by urgent telephone calls or unexpected visitors. Every Friday night we sang, in the traditional intonation, the following Saturday's portion of the law and the prophets, and so learned the synagogue cantillation by a gradual process of familiarisation — we never deliberately sat down to memorise it. From an early age I was able to sing any passage at sight. And I picked up biblical Hebrew by translating hundreds of passages in no sort of order and with no sort of system; I just found myself eventually able to read with understanding almost any part of the Hebrew Bible. To this day, if I am asked (as I occasionally am) how much Hebrew I know, I find it difficult to answer: it has often turned out that I know more than I think I know. Every now and again my father would decide that we did not know enough systematic Hebrew grammar and would bring in from his study a dusty copy of Gesenius's Hebrew grammar and ask us to memorise the paradigms of verbs. But he would never stay long at this sort of thing. In the same sporadic way he would decide suddenly that it was time Lionel and I learned some Talmud, and he would appear with one of the huge volumes and take us at a galloping pace through *Baba Mezia*, 'the Middle Gate', with its famous opening deciding the proper legal procedure and judgment if two men simultaneously come across and seize upon a lost garment ('really seize it', comments Rashi in

his commentary on the commentary on the legal core of
the passage). Or he would have a spell at mediaeval Hebrew
poetry, or at Rashi's commentary on the Pentateuch (by
some odd freak of memory I can still reel off the opening sentences of Rashi on Genesis): and once he thrust on me
a Hebrew translation of Eugene Sue's *Mysteries of Paris*. He
always professed himself surprised that we did not know
more than we did, forgetting that as he was our teacher
the responsibility was his. Once he suddenly said to me
at dinner: 'If you were hiking in Palestine and wanted to
find a place to spend the night, how would you explain
yourself in Hebrew to a passer by?' and he laughed with
a mixture of good-nature and reproof when I said '*hayesh
po makom lagur*' (is there here a place to sojourn?) instead
of '*hayesh po makom lalun*' (is there here a place to lodge
for the night?).

At one point my mother, distressed at the lack of system
in my father's teaching of us, which she attributed to his
being too busy to attend to the matter properly, insisted
that Lionel and I should receive regular lessons from a
professional Hebrew teacher. My father, who had refused to
send us to the *cheder*, the regular Hebrew school attached to
the synagogue, of which he was headmaster, on the grounds
that we knew it all anyway and further that the rabbi's sons
should not have to go to *cheder*, resisted this proposal for
a long time, but at length found a young Hebrew teacher
who, in return for weekly lessons in rabbinics from my father,
agreed to give my brother and myself regular and systematic
Hebrew lessons. As far as I remember these lessons went on
for about a year, and were the most systematic we ever had.
We wrote regular prose compositions in modern Hebrew,
and learned our grammar thoroughly. The teacher whose
name was Abraham Chayim Gordon but whom my brother
and I called Aby Chayim and mocked mercilessly was a small
man with a dark moustache and an excitable manner, much
given to extraordinary digressions on questions of law and
logic. He once tried to convince us that, just as two negatives
make a positive, so two positives make a negative, and this

is why (he alleged), when an over-eager witness replies 'yes, yes' in answer to a question put to him instead of simply 'yes', Jewish law discounts his affirmative reply. Lionel and I tried to explain to him that logically a second affirmative could only re-affirm the first, and couldn't possibly negate it, but he remained adamant in his conviction that 'yes yes' was equivalent to 'no'. It seemed to me then, as it does now, that over-eagerness in a witness should rightly be regarded with suspicion, without the implication that a double positive makes a negative. Aby Chayim also enunciated the theory (but only as a possibility) that the name 'Shylock' in *The Merchant of Venice* derived from the Hebrew verb *sha'al*, to ask, presumably because people were always asking Shylock for money. When I suggested this to my father, he replied brusquely, 'Nonsense!' Aby Chayim was very patient with us, and took our mockery in good part, and when after a while he left for America we were sorry to see him go. But I think my father was glad when he went, not because he did not respect his ability as a Hebrew teacher, but because he resented the fact that his sons should have to have Hebrew lessons from somebody else.

When I was about twelve, my father began a series of Sunday morning lectures on the Hebrew prophets to the older boys and girls of his congregation, and as this was a more advanced course than anything taught in the *cheder* he decided that my brother and I ought to go. These lectures, which were based on the Hebrew text, consisted of an *explication de texte* interspersed with some general comments. Rather to my surprise, my father also insisted on the class memorising whole chapters of Isaiah, and offered a prize to the pupil who could memorise most. For some reason, in spite of my generally bad memory, I found it easy to memorise the rich, sounding Hebrew of the 'deutero-Isaiah' (though to my father there was only one Isaiah) and, starting with the magnificent chapter 40, learned by heart most of the remainder of the book. I forced myself to keep memorising more and more, and derived a strange excitement from doing so. Every night as I lay in

bed before falling asleep I would repeat to myself as much
as I had yet learned. It was not for the sake of the prize
that I did this, although I naturally expected that the prize
would go to me, as I knew that nobody else in the class had
memorised so much. It never occurred to me that my father
would be embarrassed at having to give the prize to his own
son, and I was indignant and hurt when, at the end of the
term, he announced that the winner was a certain boy who
had memorised about half of what I had and, further, always
recited it in what sounded to me like a horrid, expressionless
monotone. I was announced as having come second equal
with a girl who had memorised the first part of chapter 40
and recited it in an adenoidal singsong which completely
ruined the sonority of the Hebrew. The grand opening of the
chapter ('*Nachamu, nachamu ami*', 'Comfort ye, comfort ye
my people') she would pronounce '*Dechebu, dechebu, abi*',
as though she had a heavy cold and at the same time was
trying to be very genteel. The girl was known as 'Dechebu
Dechebu' in our family ever after that.

That was in 1925, the year of the opening of the Hebrew
University in Jerusalem. My father was invited to take part
in the ceremony, and was most anxious to go, but he could
not possibly afford it. At the last moment one of the wealthier
members of his congregation generously offered to stand my
father the trip, an offer which was gratefully accepted. This
was the happy springtime of the Zionist movement, and
my father, a pioneer Zionist with a high idealistic belief in
the glories of a restored Zion, was excited and inspired by
his visit to an extraordinary degree. He gave many lectures
on conditions in Palestine on his return, and it was clear
that, whatever less sympathetic eyes had observed, he had
seen nothing but healthy, enthusiastic and pious young
men and women building up their ancestral home. He
was never the kind of Zionist who believed that all Jews
ought to settle in Palestine or that Jewish life outside
Palestine was doomed to decline as Zionist ideals were
realised: he believed that a rebuilt Jewish national home
would be a source of strength and religious inspiration to

the Jews of the rest of the world. His real ambition was to see Palestine become not only a Jewish state but also a British Dominion, an integral part of the British Empire — a position which was held by some influential English political figures, led by Colonel Josiah Wedgwood (later Lord Wedgwood), who wrote a book, entitled *The Seventh Dominion*, strongly advocating such a development. Any friction between Zionists and the British Government was a source of bitter disappointment to my father, who had known and admired Lord Balfour, and the events of the 1940s shook him severely. He was shocked by the extreme position taken by some vocal American Zionists in those later years and by their tendency to condone terrorism, and at the same time he was hurt and disappointed at the behaviour of the British Government. At the time of his death, in 1945, he had moved a considerable distance away from the Zionist orthodoxy of the day and was more concerned with the position of Jews outside Palestine.

But in 1925 nothing of this was visible on the horizon, and my father's visit to Palestine was in many respects the high point of his career. He was invited to be present (if my recollection of his account of his trip has not become confused) at the laying of the foundation stone of the new Tel Aviv synagogue, and boasted that when he was unexpectedly asked to make a speech (in modern Hebrew) he was able to give an eloquent, spontaneous oration which drew great applause. The ceremony was held on the eighth day of Passover, which was observed as a festival day (when no work could be done) by those Jews who came from outside Palestine, because doubt about the calendar had, at an early stage of the Jewish dispersion, led Jews of the *galuth* (exile) to observe an extra day in order to be on the safe side; but it was not observed by those Jews who lived in Palestine, for whom Passover had concluded the day before. The result was that the Jews from abroad, like my father, were unable to ride or write or work on that day, while the Jews of Tel Aviv went about their daily affairs in the normal way. Some of those attending the ceremony at the synagogue were thus still in festival mood, and others were not. My father used to talk about this with an amused air, as reflecting an interesting facet of modern Jewish life; he remarked also that it meant that he, unlike the other speakers on this occasion, who lived in Palestine, was unable to write down notes for his speech and would have had to deliver it without notes even if he had not preferred to do so anyway.

Everything on this Palestine expedition seemed to go well. The only fly in the ointment was that my father was accompanied throughout his visit by a somewhat eccentric gentleman, an Edinburgh Christadelphian, who professed himself a great friend of the Jews and an ardent Zionist. This gentleman (who tacked himself on to my father in order to make sure that he would have the entrée to all the proper places) was a great bore who enjoyed the sound of his own voice and edited (or perhaps only distributed in Scotland) a strange magazine called *Glad Tidings of the Coming Age*, which he sent regularly to my father. He used to make speeches to Jewish audiences in Edinburgh in which he announced that he was converted to Zionism in Norfolk, Virginia, where someone had once said to him: 'If there is anything of the milk of human kindness in you, you will become a Zionist.' Apparently he found this argument so convincing that he became a Zionist forthwith. He frequented Jewish homes in Edinburgh and occasionally came to the synagogue; his Jewish contacts resulted in his picking up a few Hebrew words, which he tended to pronounce with the letters transposed, spooneristically, as it were. He would call *shekolim* (shekels; specifically, in Zionist usage, the silver coin — in Britain, half-a-crown — which each Zionist paid to the movement in token of his membership) *shelokim*, and would make speeches about *shelokim* on Zionist platforms. He was an object of ribald mirth among the Jewish youth of Edinburgh, and was something of a thorn in my father's flesh as he tagged around after him in Palestine. Jews are vulnerable to that kind of lunatic pro-Semitism; they cannot afford to reject it, but its acceptance is often embarrassing.

A more congenial pro-Semitic gentile in Edinburgh was the white bearded Mr Hogg, a kindly old man who would attend the synagogue fairly frequently and was on friendly terms with many Jewish families. Once at a children's *Chanukah* party he asked one of the young guests what *Chanukah* was all about, expecting to hear the familiar story of Judas Maccabeus and the rededication of the Temple, and was horrified when the child replied: '*Chanukah* is the Jews' Christmas.' The story was told as a joke among the Jews of Edinburgh, but I remember my father looked thoughtful when he heard it: did it suggest, perhaps, the instability of his synthesis?

We used to have quite a number of non-Jewish visitors to the synagogue, mostly Presbyterian ministers and divinity students. Many of them would take off their hats as they entered, to the scandal of the congregation, who would motion the offending Gentile to replace his hat, sometimes gesturing so violently that the poor man would be quite confused and not know what he was supposed to do. (Orthodox Jews, of course, always cover their heads when they pray or engage in biblical or talmudic study.) I was quick to notice these visitors, and to resent for their sake the lack of decorum and haphazard out-of-time singing so characteristic of an orthodox Jewish congregation. I would wish that everyone would behave with a ritual solemnity so as to impress the newcomer. It was years later that I learned to understand and appreciate the ease and individualism with which the orthodox Jew conducts himself in the presence of his Maker, and to resent not the lack of decorum in orthodox congregations but the artificial stiffness and coldness of certain less orthodox services. As a child I was always annoyed by the lack of manners displayed by the older members of my father's congregation, and my father, too, worked hard to improve the discipline of the service. He at least put a stop to the continuous walking in and out and the perpetual chattering, but even he could not get the older men to suspend their individualistic habits, such as singing one bar ahead of the *chazan* to show that they knew the words and music better than he did, or engaging in loud private prayer during what was supposed to be a hushed pause in the service. One thing, however, I was never ashamed of when there was a visitor present, and that was my father's sermon. When my father moved into the pulpit to preach, I would say to myself: '*Now* he'll see what a Jewish rabbi can do,' and I would watch the visitor's face for signs that he was moved and impressed as my father spoke. And my father never let me down: he was a great preacher, and, without the aid of any kind of note, could build up from exposition of the day's text through illustrative anecdote to a climax of eloquence I have rarely heard equalled. He gave out the text in Hebrew, and then translated it into English, continuing his sermon in the latter language. Sometimes, on a chill winter morning when there were not more than a dozen people present, most of them old men whose command of the English language was rudimentary, I would feel that nobody except myself understood or appreciated his preaching, and a sense of the waste of it all would press sadly upon me. For my father preached every sabbath, however small the congregation might be; and his sermon was always perfectly constructed, always cogently and eloquently expressed, always sounding with true moral passion. Only once do I remember his not preaching (apart from the very few occasions when he was absent through illness); and that was on a cold February morning when the primitive central heating apparatus had broken down and there was barely a *minyan* (ten men) present. On that occasion he reluctantly decided to let his shivering congregation go home twenty minutes earlier than usual, and did not preach. I said to him on the way home that I missed his sermon, and I remember his sudden pleased smile as he turned to me and said: 'Did you?'

CHAPTER THREE

In March 1919, at the age of six and a half, I went with
my father to interview Mr John Alison, headmaster of
George Watson's Boys' College, Edinburgh. The interview
was satisfactory, and the same day (unless my memory
telescopes the events) I took my seat in Class 'B' of the
elementary department. The classroom was tucked away in
the extreme corner of the right wing of the school building;
you had to turn into a small L-shaped recess in order to
get there. The characteristic school smell — it seemed to
be a mixture of wood, chalk, leather (from school bags),
ink (the school ink was almost black and had a pungent
odour) and the monastic coolness which emanated from
the stone-floored corridors — assailed my nostrils as I came
in at the main entrance with my father, up the wide steps by
the portico and the fluted columns, past the janitors' room
where we were directed to the headmaster by a uniformed
official with twinkling blue eyes and a small white beard. (I
was to know him well later; he was Willie, the senior janitor,
good friend to all the small boys of Watson's. Fairlie, the
junior janitor, was of more unpredictable temper. The fact
that Fairlie was universally known by his surname while
Willie was just Willie to everybody indicated a significant
difference in their characters. Willie retired half way through
my school career at Watson's, and for years afterwards I used
to see the brisk old man with a single golf club in his hand
— a cleek — on his way to Bruntsfield Links to knock a
ball round the simple nine-hole free golfcourse there.)

I found the work in Class 'B' easy enough, for I could
already read and write and do simple sums with slapdash

speed, but it took me some time to get used to the formality
and regularity of the classroom. For some reason, the idea
of starting work promptly at nine o'clock each morning
distressed me, and I explained to Miss Don, the teacher,
that I did not think I should be able to manage it. She
smiled, and said that I must do my best, and I earnestly
replied that I would. Shortly afterwards, Miss Don left
to get married and her place was taken by Miss Barron
or Miss Barrons, a name which the boys in the class for
some reason found themselves unable to enunciate clearly.
Miss Barn, Miss Barmy, and Miss Barley were favourite
variants, and I remember myself that when I first heard
her called Miss Barley I decided at once that that was the
simplest and most convenient form of the name and that
I would therefore stick to it. I do not think that there was
any deliberate mockery involved in this playing about with
Miss Barron's name: 'Barron' just seemed to be difficult
or at least implausible.

In the Autumn of 1919 I moved up to Class 'D', taught
by one of the numerous Miss Smiths at Watson's. She
was popularly known among the boys as 'Smiggles o' D',
which distinguished her from 'Smiggles of H', the Miss
Smith who was to teach me the following year when I
moved up into Class 'H'. Smiggles o' D was an old
war-horse of a teacher, who had got the teaching of
seven- and eight-year-olds systematised into a well-tried
routine. She was efficient in a tired sort of way, and had
a cut-and-dried list of basic offences for which punishment
by the tawse (a leather strap, used on the palm of the hand)
was obligatory. If, for example, you handed in your writing
exercise (which was done at home) smudged and filthy with
dirty finger marks you got the tawse. And of course you
got the tawse for cheating. One morning, after she had
marked the sums that we had been doing in class, she
discovered that both I and the boy sitting next to me had
got one sum wrong, and that we both had the same wrong
answer. She decided that I had copied my answer from
the boy beside me. This decision outraged me, for in fact

I had not copied the answer, and I was better at arithmetic than the boy whom she assumed I had copied from. She insisted that the evidence proved that I had cheated, yet, since she refrained from giving me the tawse and contented herself with a tongue lashing, she must have realised that there was just as much chance of the other boy's having cheated. (As a matter of fact, I was convinced then and I still am that neither of us cheated: our getting the same wrong answer was simply a coincidence.) Throughout the rest of the day she would interrupt what she was saying to refer to me as the boy who had cheated. After a while I ceased to deny it, and, with the extraordinary resilience of childhood, shrugged the whole thing off. But I knew from that moment that Miss Smith was a wickedly irresponsible woman, and I never forgave her. I cannot bring myself to forgive her yet, though she has been dead now for some years. She destroyed forever my trust in teachers.

The following year, when I was in Class 'H', I really did cheat, in a curiously light-hearted way without any sense of sin. It still puzzles me why I did it. One day I could not be bothered memorising my Geography homework, so I carefully wrote out the names of the rivers and the populations of the cities and the other facts and figures I was expected to learn by heart, and when next morning we were asked to write down the answers to questions on these matters I quietly took out the piece of paper on which I had written down the answers and copied them into my exercise book. As far as I can remember, I made no great effort to conceal what I was doing, and congratulated myself on having discovered a simple and efficient way of getting good marks. Of course I was soon spotted, and Smiggles of H was horrified at my criminal behaviour — all the more criminal because I was regarded as a bright boy who had no need of such wicked tricks. I got two strokes of the tawse — my first experience of that instrument of torture — and was sent to the bottom of the class. I felt neither worried nor aggrieved, moving through the whole experience in a sort of trance, but I was astonished at the amount of real pain inflicted by the tawse and by the length of time it lasted. For over half an hour my hand felt as though it were about a foot thick and the tips of my fingers, which felt as large as balloons, pulsed with agony. Then suddenly the pain changed into a warm glow, and everything was very pleasant. I never bore any grudge against Smiggles of H; she was, of course, only doing her duty.

My father, satisfied that he had started my brother Lionel and myself at a good school, took little interest in the details of our secular education in these early years. This was partly because he was too busy: these were the years when he was licking his congregation into shape and establishing himself in Edinburgh and throughout Scotland as an important public figure and recognised spokesman for the Jewish point of view; and it was at this time, too, that my mother had her serious illness. Another reason for his relative indifference to what we were doing in the elementary school at Watson's was that he had nothing to say about this stage of our education. He was waiting until he could cap quotations from Homer with us or ask what book of Virgil we were reading or for that still later stage when he could inquire whether we had read Buckle on the history of civilisation or David Hume on human nature. He did, however, appear at the annual school prize-giving, in dignified black coat and silk hat, to have a few grave words with Dr Alison (he became 'Dr Alison' in, I think, 1922, when Edinburgh University granted him an honorary LL.D.) and thank him for what the school was doing for 'my boys'.

Watson's was divided into three sections, the elementary school, the junior school, and the senior school. I entered the junior school at the age of nine, after leaving Class 'H'. Here we still had one teacher for all subjects, and for the first two years they were still women teachers. But in the autumn of 1923, when I entered the third year of the junior school, I came under the redoubtable 'Dub-Dub', Mr W.W. Anderson, a man with a reputation throughout the school as a stern disciplinarian and a teacher of old-fashioned strictness and thoroughness. He was within

a few years of retirement when I came to know him as a
teacher, a dour old Scot with a grey and ginger moustache
and very little hair. His methods were old fashioned, but
remarkably effective. He battered the boys with a brand of
irony all his own, and after bellowing at one of them for some
error or piece of forgetfulness he would lean back against
the mantel and say sardonically: 'You think I'm hard on
you, don't you? You think I'm a Turk? You think I'm a
Tartar? You're going to complain to your parents about
me?' He would then pause and remove his gold-rimmed
pince-nez glasses. 'Go home and tell your mother I'm a
Tartar. Tell her I'm a Turk.' And he would give a curious
little sibilant titter which sounded like 'sih, sih, sih'.

Dub-Dub never used the tawse, but he had his own way
of keeping discipline. He was more feared, I think, than any
other master in the school, and it was rumoured among the
boys that he was not allowed to use the strap because once,
away back in the 1880s or '90s, he had broken a boy's
wrist with it. But I doubt if this was true. His moods of
sternness made one tremble, and his levity had something
of the quality of a jocund rattlesnake. He could get the
most extraordinary effects out of the simplest sentences.
If he threatened (as he occasionally did) to throw a boy
out of the class-room, he would say, in a peculiarly intense
intonation, 'I'll change your name to Walker.' That threat,
with its monstrous pun (it meant 'I'll make you walk out
of the room') always hushed a class to immediate stillness.
'Change it to Walker,' he'd repeat, meditatively. Then,
suddenly: 'Give your dear mother my compliments and
tell her I'm a Turk.'

He taught by slogans, rhyming tags, and rules chanted
to the accompaniment of a waved pointer. (Do all school
teachers employ the pointer to the extent that the Watson's
teachers did in those days? It was their favourite weapon, and
I have a mental image of every one of them, each holding the
pointer in his favourite attitude, one pointing to a wall map,
another waving it in the air, a third banging it on the floor,
a fourth following the lines of some geometrical figure on

the blackboard with it, a fifth poking it in an inattentive boy's stomach. And one senior teacher used to lay it across his back and wrap his arms round it, wrestling with it and himself as he talked.) One of his favourite grammatical rules was that which postulates the nominative case after the verb 'to be', and if anybody said, for example, '*Marcus est puerum*' instead of '*Marcus est puer*' he would at once break into a wild chant, waving the pointer at the offender, and digging it into his stomach at the end:

> Before and after the verb 'to be'
> The very same cases I shall see —
> IF I keep my eyes open.

He was intensely proud of being Scottish, but his Scotland was not that of the sentimental Jacobites or of the modern Scottish Nationalists. The view of Scottish history that he taught us was the Calvinist–Nationalist one. No nonsense about Mary Queen of Scots or Bonnie Prince Charlie for him; it was the Covenanters and the Battle of Bothwell Brig and the horrid persecutions of Bloody Claverhouse that we learned about. We had to memorise the oath that the Covenanters took, and were liable to be called upon to recite it at any time. Though his geographical interests were wide, and we were expected to know a great deal about French rivers ('the Rhone joins the *Sone* [Saone] at *Lyone* [Lyon], was one of his rhyming tags) and German towns, history for him was always and only Scottish history, and almost exclusively the history of the Covenanters at that. The only boy's book that won his approval was R.M. Ballantyne's *Hunted and Harried* (less well known in its day than the same author's *Coral Island*), which dealt in a tone of idealising sympathy with the sufferings of the upholders of the true Kirk. I persuaded my father that it was one of our required schoolbooks, so that he bought it for me; I carried it around with me at school conspicuously, and Dub-Dub nodded approval.

Dub-Dub had an elaborate system of marking his pupils. The order in which you sat in class was determined by how well you did, and at the end of the day he gave five marks to the boy sitting at the top, four marks to the second boy, three to the third, two to the fourth, and one to the fifth. The next day the previous day's five top boys moved right down to the bottom (whence of course they tried to work their way up to the top again) and everybody else moved up automatically five places. The competition was tremendous, and the movements up and down continuous. Dub-Dub would shoot a question at the class, starting with the top boy and going down until he could find a boy who answered it correctly (and immediately); that boy would then go up top, and everybody else between the winning boy's original seat and the top would move down one. 'Take him down!' he would roar, as two or three boys missed a question and he came to one who got it right. He would give you only a split second to answer. Pouncing anywhere in the class his pointer would travel down, 'Next, next, next — right! Take him down!' A 'taking down' session was liable to start at any moment throughout the school day, and sometimes the excitement was furious. Dub-Dub particularly enjoyed humiliating a bright boy. He would wait until one of these was momentarily dozing or looking out of the window and lunge at him with his pointer. 'Accusative plural of *acies*. Next, next, next — TAKE HIM DOWN!'

This was more than sport, for one's weekly marks depended in considerable measure on one's daily place in class, and out of one's weekly marks (together with periodical tests and examinations) was figured one's final position in class at the end of the year. The boys in the top half-dozen positions got book prizes, and the boy at the very top got a scholarship, which meant that his parents had no fees to pay during the following year. It was in Dub-Dub's class that I first became fully sensible of the tremendously competitive atmosphere of a Scottish school. The curriculum and the teaching were really organised for the boys at the top of the class, and at every test and examination relative positions were worked out and hopes rose and fell. More than half of the class were out of the battle; they lived a more relaxed and I suppose a happier life, content if they could keep abreast of the work sufficiently to be promoted into a higher class at the end of the year. But for those in the running for awards, the competition was keen and unremitting.

Of course there were other ways of winning fame at school, notably on the rugby field. But that way was completely closed to me, not because I was naturally incompetent at sport (though I never liked organised games of any kind) but because games were played on Saturday, the Jewish sabbath, and my playing then was quite out of the question. I suppose I could have found a way of taking part in practices while not playing in matches, but my father's complete lack of awareness of this side of school life, and his tacit assumption that school was where one learned the orthodox academic subjects and nothing else prevented this. Not for him any notion that games built up character: his children's characters would be formed by the atmosphere of a Jewish home, and the school had no responsibility for that. He was simply puzzled or bored if anyone showed interest in competitive sport. Exercise was another matter. He believed in taking long walks over the hills; he understood and approved when, during my university days, I went with my fellow students for rambles over the Pentland Hills or spent part of the holidays hiking in the Highlands; swimming, too, he considered healthful, and golf was an exercise that both promoted health and gave one the opportunity of moving among fine scenery. But rugby or cricket did not exist for him, and so he assumed that they did not exist for his children.

It would not be strictly true to say that I resented this; it was a situation that I took absolutely for granted, as part of the natural order of things. I had no great desire to play rugger or cricket, but I did at times feel embarrassed at being the only boy in my class who was totally ignorant even of the terminology connected with these games. And I knew nothing about the school matches: they were nearly all played on Saturdays and Lionel and I rarely saw one. But my mother, so much more sensitive to this aspect of school life than my father, realised that we were missing something and always found out from the local paper whenever a match was scheduled to be played on a weekday. She would give us the information and pack us off to Myreside, the school playing field. In this way we sometimes saw the opening match of the Watsonians (Watson's former pupils) against Hillhead F.P.S, generally played, if I remember rightly, on the first Thursday before the beginning of the Autumn term. And sometimes a match was postponed because of the weather or some other reason, and we would get a half holiday on a Wednesday to go and see the re-play: the whole school would troop out to Myreside, and Lionel and I would follow, not quite knowing what it was all about — indeed not at first knowing where Myreside was, something we dared not admit as we blindly followed the crowd — but trying to look nonchalant and well informed. We could not enter for the annual School Sports either, because this great event was also held on a Saturday. It was only late in my school career that I discovered that I was a good sprinter, and could out-run many of my school fellows who had some reputation as athletes. But there was nothing I could do about it.

There was one compensating factor, however. It was during my year in Dub-Dub's class that I had begun to amuse myself by writing crude and highly derivative verses. I found that I had a certain facility in handling rhyme and metre, and in the imitative way of childhood I turned out a number of descriptions of imaginary moonlit scenes and similar things. It never occurred to me at this time that this was in the least interesting or unusual, that it was any different from scribbling in a drawing book or playing a parlour game: I remember my astonishment at discovering some years later, when our English teacher set us a verse writing competition, that most of the boys in my class found difficulty in putting a thought into rhymed, metrical verse. If occasionally I read out one of my poems to the family, I did so in the same casual way that one might show a trick with a match box or demonstrate that one could now turn a proper somersault. It was generally humorous poems that I read to the family, like 'The Rime of the Ancient Scavenger' and a set of Lewis Carroll-like nonsense verses entitled 'The Polywagoo'.

In my second-last year at school I translated the first book of the *Odyssey* into limerick verse. All I remember now is the opening:

> Tell me, O Muse, of the chap
> Who wandered all over the map.
>   This remarkable boy
>   After bashing down Troy
> Started off on a tour of mishap.

It was done in the same spirit as other boys made catapults or collected cigarette cards.

It was my father who first began to take my verses seriously. When I was eleven years old he bought me a notebook in which to write out fair copies, and after I had gone to bed he would solemnly read what I had written there and make minor corrections to improve the regularity of the metre (and once, I remember, to correct the grammar). One evening he sat down with me and gave me a lesson in metrics, explaining to me about the various feet, and writing out metrical schemes with u's and dashes ($\cup - \cup -$). He had the strictest notions of poetic rhythm, and knew nothing of the doctrine of equivalence or the sprung rhythm theories of Hopkins. Nevertheless, his discipline was helpful to me at the time: it gave me a sense of technical craftsmanship and chastened my uncontrolled exuberance. It also gave me a bias in favour of metrical regularity which persists to this day.

One day, without my knowledge, my father brought my notebook of poems to school and showed it to Dr Alison, who referred him to Mr Findlay ('Henry John'), the head of the English department in the senior school. Mr Findlay liked some of the poems, and chose one ('To a fountain in moonlight', describing in a fairly complicated verse form a scene I had never witnessed) to print in *The Watsonian*, the school magazine. *The Watsonian* was a dull, business-like magazine, with contributions by masters and by senior boys; unlike some school magazines, it had no children's section in which to print crude and amusing effusions by youngsters. My poem, therefore, was not printed as an amusing or psychologically interesting example of a child's versifying: it was printed as a poem in its own right. I was both pleased and embarrassed. It was embarrassing to have my father talking about my poems and showing them to teachers and it was even embarrassing, in a way, to see something from my private notebook in print, to be read by my schoolfellows. But of course I was also immensely proud — proud of my printed poem, and proud of my father's interest in my verses.

Dub-Dub was not impressed. One day, after the appearance of the issue of the *The Watsonian* which contained my poem, he found me looking dreamily out of the window and at once proceeded to catch me out in a 'taking down' session. After my humiliation he growled at me: 'I hope you're not letting all this poetry stuff addle your brains and keep you from your proper work.' The class tittered, and I was profoundly hurt.

I was eleven years old then, and the next year I moved up to the senior school, where the organisation was quite different and we had a different master for each subject. We started Science this year (with Physics) and French and Algebra and Geometry, and in History for the first time we moved away from Scotland to get a wider perspective. It was now that I began to prefer some subjects to others: English, History and Languages were my favourites, while Mathematics (except Algebra, which for some reason I liked and was reasonably good at) and Physics (which was badly taught by the master we had then, though there were some excellent Physics teachers in the school) I found on the whole rather dull. The first year of the senior school had I suppose about a hundred and forty boys, and they were divided into four groups: IA, a group of about thirty-five, contained the brightest boys, IB the next brightest, and IC the poorer pupils, while in I Mod (later called ID) were the boys who elected to take the 'modern' side as a preparation for a non-professional future — in my time they were regarded as a pretty inferior lot. I was in IA, and the next year moved into IIA, and so on. Here the competition was extremely fierce, and for my first two years in the senior school I stayed about tenth — which meant missing a prize or a scholarship. Each time I started the year determined that I would work really hard and come top of the class, but somehow that pristine keenness evaporated as the academic year progressed: I worked well at the subjects I liked, and tended to ignore the others. In my third senior year we began Greek, which meant that I was now taking three languages, Latin, French and Greek. (Normally, one had to choose at this stage between Greek and French, dropping the latter if one was taking up the former, but Mr Robertson, the new headmaster who had succeeded Dr Alison, tried an experiment this year: he had the brightest boys of the year — those in the A class — take both Greek and French, without giving them any choice.) This gave me an extra subject which I liked and was good at, and meant that out of the eight subjects I took I was top or near the top in five (English, History, Latin, Greek, and French), though I remained about the middle in the other three (Science, Mathematics and Geography). The result was that one exciting day early in July 1927, I dashed home across the Meadows during the lunch interval to announce to my parents that I had won a 'bursary' — that is, remission of fees for the ensuing year, together with a cash grant. I had not in fact come top of my class, for there were several bursaries available for the third year and of course IIIA captured them all, but I had finally got into the scholarship category and I was immensely pleased and excited.

I was pleased on my own account, of course, but even more because I knew my parents would be gratified. At this time I had formed an image of my father as a lonely idealist who would be sustained by the knowledge that one at least of his children was of a similar habit of mind. (My brother Lionel took his schooling with a lazy matter-of-factness and was content to swim gently along in the middle of a

B stream. It was much later that his specific talents — legal and rhetorical — began to display themselves.) I believed that if I could show my father signs that I was on the way to becoming a serious thinker and writer and linguist, or at any rate someone of moral and intellectual distinction, it would sweeten his whole life. As a matter of fact, I found myself developing an almost paternal attitude towards both my parents. Looking at them sitting by the fire on a Friday night, tired after a hard week's work, love and pity would well up within me and I wanted to say something that would give them tremendous pleasure. It is easy to see why I felt protective towards my mother: she had had periods of serious illness and I felt that her arduous daily routine of housework might at any moment break her. On the rare occasions when she went out in the evening to some social function, I would lie awake in bed until she got safely home, thinking of her as someone too fragile to be out in the dark night, especially if there was a high wind or the weather was really cold. It is more surprising that I should have felt in a somewhat similar way towards my father, for he was a man of fine physique and great strength of character whom one would not for a moment have associated with any kind of weakness. Underneath this strength, however, I seemed to detect even at this early age a certain child-like quality of character, a naïve faith in the world, a simple conviction of the absolute rightness of his own position, that made me want to protect him from certain kinds of knowledge and to keep on reassuring him that the world was indeed as he saw it and we were all on his side. He knew nothing, I would sometimes feel, of the realities of the modern world, of its daily, trivial preoccupations. Could such a man know that schoolboys talked smut, that to many parents as well as to many boys sport meant more than study, that stealing notebooks from the janitor's cupboard at school was regarded by almost everybody as legitimate, that most people were silly, cruel, materialist, selfish? His eloquent and stirring sermons, which I so admired, did not really belong to the world in which I moved at school and when in the Edinburgh streets. Could he know that the ritual of orthodox Judaism, so important and impressive to him (and to me), was comic or fatuous to many people? The thinker, the scholar, the idealist, were isolated characters, who had no part in the life of the rough mob. It was at this time that I refused to go to parties and preferred to sit at home and read poetry or go for lonely walks in which I worked myself up into a state of romantic exaltation. Lonely myself, feeling different from and (it must be admitted) superior to other people, I saw my father as another lonely hero, but one who was not really aware of his essential loneliness, one who did not know how different the world really was from his noble vision of it.

Looking back, it seems to me now that in some ways I exaggerated my father's innocence. He was in many respects remarkably tough-minded. He had an uncanny gift for recognising imposters; and his duties as rabbi naturally brought him into contact with sordid aspects of, for example, marriage that as a child I knew nothing whatever about. Yet I still think that my general impression of him as an innocent and lonely idealist was essentially right. In spite of his knowledge of the seamy side of life, in spite of his shrewdness in detecting imposture and his toughness in handling dishonest appeals for charity, a certain childish optimism was central to his character. Another childish trait of his was a naïve susceptibility to flattery. Anybody could disarm him with a compliment. Though he found it hard to suffer fools gladly, a man who in all other ways appeared a fool could earn a reputation for wisdom with my father by telling him how much he admired his letters to *The Scotsman* or what a wonderful speaker he thought he was. I remember once, after I was grown up, arguing with him about the intelligence of a young man who had had occasion to visit the house and had talked a great deal of arrant nonsense. 'Oh, he's not such a fool,' my father said, and added, with a smile of reminiscent pleasure, 'He said that my letters to the editor were the best things that ever appeared in *The Scotsman* and I ought to collect them in a book.' There was something rather engaging about this simple kind of vanity.

There can be no doubt of my father's loneliness, though he would have been surprised to hear of it. His own work as rabbi and synthesiser of orthodox Jewish and British culture so engrossed him, both physically and mentally, that he had no time for the luxuries of friendship or society. His social life was crowded indeed, but it was part of his professional life, and the weddings, receptions, public meetings, official dinners and similar functions which he attended in enormous numbers could hardly be put in the category of relaxation with friends. My impression was that the nearest he ever came to relaxing outside his own home was at Masonic dinners: he was a keen Mason, and enjoyed the meetings of Lodge Solomon (of which he was a Past Master) which included both Jewish and Christian members. But he had no real cronies. Throughout his whole adult life there was no one outside his immediate family with whom he was on first-name terms. There were several members of his congregation with whom he would enjoy a chat on community or general affairs. But there was no one with whom he was really intimate, no one who understood fully what he was trying to do, what his concept of Scottish–Jewish life was, what constituted the real centre of his moral and emotional life. Even my mother hardly ever called him 'Salis'. She once told me that she was relieved when her first child was born because it solved the problem of what to call her husband, whom she felt shy of calling by his (admittedly somewhat unusual) first name: she called him 'Daddy' more often than not from that time on. He always called her 'Flora', with the 'o' vowel rather clipped and short.

It was this sort of thing that I was becoming more and more aware of in my fifteenth year, which I look back on as a critical year in my development. I remember 1927 — particularly the summer — with especial clarity. It was the year of my first bursary, the year when I wrote a vast amount of derivative verse and cultivated moods of introspective melancholy. How can I explain the enormous sense of emotional excitement which used to overcome me as I sat on summer evenings by the window of the attic room Lionel and I used as a 'study' and responded to the sights and sounds of Edinburgh life outside? I was the artist, pondering over the sad beauty of human destiny. When I read Wordsworth's phrase, 'the still sad music of humanity', I thought I recognised at once what he meant. To this day I associate that phrase with my brooding over those summer evenings from my attic window in Millerfield Place. These experiences are not merely fragments that linger in my memory: they are as vivid today as they ever were, an important part of myself. But though the memories are still vivid and important to me, the experience itself, which recurred frequently throughout my teens and my twenties, came less and less in my thirties and now, in my forties, I find that it has gone apparently for good.

It was in my fifteenth year, too, that I became aware of a difference in character and temperament between my mother and my father which led me, with the naïve confidence of childhood, to feel that I understood them both better than either understood the other, and I wished to interpret them to each other. I would imagine my father's youth and his student days in Germany (somehow always connected with a picture in a German reading book of a late nineteenth-century German railway station, with men in top hats and beards walking about or sitting waiting for a train: this picture seemed to me infinitely sad, suggesting a lost world and symbolising in some oblique way the lonely self-dedication with which my father lived and worked in the years before I was born). I would think of my mother, the beautiful eldest daughter of a Liverpool Jewish family, musical, literary, accomplished, marrying my father at the age of nineteen in a splendour of idealistic hope that she would absorb his knowledge and power and the two would serve the great cause together. My mother's idealism was nineteenth-century romantic, while my father's was eighteenth-century sentimental, and in spite of their deep mutual affection there were important points on which they never (or so it seemed to me) really understood each other. Mother used to tell us that just before her marriage she had anticipated that once married to a brilliant rabbi she would of course be taught by him and become something so much more than the housekeeper and nursemaid that most wives were content to be. But my father was disconcerted with my mother's vision of herself and by her ambition to pursue her artistic and intellectual life after marriage; with the best will in the world and with all the affection in the world he remained puzzled by the frustration which occasionally rose up in her and found vent in some unexpected word or action. He was proud of his wife's accomplishments, but his view of a wife was essentially the old-fashioned Jewish one of the 'woman of worth' and he never really appreciated what my mother had given up on marriage.

I suppose it is uncommon for a child of fifteen or so to feel in some respects paternal towards his parents, especially when one of the parents is at the same time a symbol of strength and dignity, but to me it was a characteristic feeling and coloured my childhood from early adolescence. Walking with my father to the synagogue on a Saturday morning I would search my mind for something to say which I felt would encourage him. I reported to him anything flattering that my schoolmasters had said, not by way of boasting but to make him feel happy about me, and on a few occasions I made up things to tell him which I thought would help him to remain convinced that the world was going as he believed and wanted it to go. Similarly, when I came into the kitchen and found my mother occupied with some domestic task there, I would try to find something to say that would please and cheer her. This was more difficult, for my mother was (or seemed to me) an emotionally more complicated person. To my father, I thought that anything I could say which indicated that a world of enlightened moral idealism was showing increased respect for the Jewish people and their religion, or that people I had met had read and approved something he had written, or that I myself was developing so as eventually to play my part with dignity and credit in the Anglo-Jewish or Scoto-Jewish world — anything of this sort would please and cheer him (as I am sure it did). But to find the properly cheering words for my mother was a more difficult business, and in talking with her I often ended by displaying my own problems, something I do not remember once doing with my father.

This may help to explain why I considered my winning a school bursary in the summer of 1927 as something that was significant largely as a contribution to my parents' happiness. It is possible that I exaggerated the importance they attached to scholastic achievement and that I was attributing to them an attitude which I had partly absorbed from the competitive atmosphere of school itself and partly deduced from my father's own career and character as well as from the traditional Jewish (and, for that matter, also Scottish) attitude towards academic success; but there can at least be no doubt of the financial relief it must have been to my father to be saved from having to pay even the relatively small fees they charged at Watson's. After 1927 I won a bursary annually, and in my last year at school won a scholarship that carried me through Edinburgh University, so that henceforth my education did not cost my father anything. The fact that I was contributing to lessening the financial strain under which he continually laboured gave me great satisfaction.

Life was fairly hard during my last four years at school. We had a considerable amount of homework to do, which was supposed to take about two hours but often (if I was wrestling with a complicated mathematical exercise, for example) took longer. Then I was taking both piano and (after 1926) violin lessons, which involved practising daily. Of course I skimped my practising, and often did little more than look over the week's assignment the day before my lesson, but still, having practising as one of the things down on the list to be done, I could not feel free of an evening if I had not done it. We were supposed to do some Hebrew daily as well, as a rule prepare a piece of biblical translation in which my father examined Lionel and myself on Friday nights. Sometimes in the summer term I would be able to do my homework, my practising of both piano and violin and my Hebrew in a reasonably short time and feel myself free to spend the rest of the afternoon and the evening as I pleased. This, however, was so unusual that I still remember some of the occasions when it happened and recall the sense of freedom and self-righteousness with which I went out to play in the Meadows with all my day's work done. Generally I went around with a sense of duty undone, for I often left homework uncompleted and the piano and violin untouched.

I liked music and was anxious to become proficient, but I had a fatal facility which enabled me to improvise and 'mess about' instead of learning the hard way, so that I never developed the skill I could and should have acquired. My piano teacher was an interesting and able woman, Miss Lucy Brown, who came to the house one afternoon a week to give me my lesson. Over the years we developed a real friendship, and often we would sit and talk about my ambitions for the future or the pleasures of the different seasons or music and poetry, or indeed anything at all. Miss Brown was one of those spinster music teachers, so common throughout the country, with real talent but not sufficient to enable them to become professional performers, who eke out a bare living by giving weekly lessons to schoolchildren. Her life was a fairly grim struggle, and as she trotted wearily around from one pupil to another she must have found her profession profoundly disappointing. She had a tiny flat in Alva Street, at the West End, and one day when she had hurt her ankle and could not walk she asked me to come there for my lesson. When I arrived I found that, having just washed her hair, she had it loose behind her back, and looked young and pretty. For the first time I realised that Miss Brown was a woman, and not merely a music teacher with some interesting ideas. Her old upright piano was in poor shape, and she apologised for it. Her flat was shabby and showed clearly the hardness of her struggle. I went away from that lesson (I was fifteen or sixteen at the time) seeing Miss Brown as a tragic, romantic figure, a beautiful and talented woman beaten down by harsh circumstances and facing a future of loneliness and poverty. When I left school I continued with the violin but, realising that I would not have the time to work at two instruments any longer, I gave up taking piano lessons. Miss Brown and I parted with reluctance. I think she was genuinely fond of me and had hoped that our weekly talks would continue. I thought of her often during my university years. In my final year at the university one of my fellow students told me that he wanted to begin taking piano lessons and I gave him Miss Brown's name and address. He wrote to her and he told me the following week that his letter had been returned marked 'Deceased'. Miss Brown, as I discovered later, had been suffering from a fatal malady when I had taken my farewell of her, though of course I knew nothing of it at the time.

When I think of Miss Brown now I think of our drawing-room at Millerfield Place where I would have my lesson at four-thirty on Monday afternoons. The drawing-room was not often used during the week. On Sunday afternoons in the winter a fire was lit there, and we generally had a family evening there with music on Sunday evening. Otherwise it was left unheated except for a small electric heater which was switched on whenever anyone went up to practise. (I say 'went up' because the drawing-room was upstairs, on the first floor.) It was a large, fairly handsome room, with a white marble (or imitation marble? I always thought of it as marble) fireplace, some Constable reproductions on the walls, and in one corner the old Ernst Kapps grand piano that my father had bought second-hand for my mother on their honeymoon for £27.10s. Lionel or Sylvia would bring Miss Brown up a cup of tea soon after she arrived, and she would sit sipping it beside the piano while I went through my scales and arpeggios. My father, who generally took a nap from about three o'clock until half-past four, would often leave his stiff white artificial cuffs standing on a little table in the drawing-room, and then come in to collect them when Miss Brown was there, forgetting that this was Monday and she would be giving me my lesson. He knew I was there, of course, by the sound of the piano, but thought I was just practising. He would get up from his rest and refresh himself by washing his face in cold water (he always washed with a great deal of splashing and spluttering). Then he would barge into the drawing-room (which was next to the bathroom) to collect his cuffs, breathing heavily after his cold water wash. He would be well inside the room before he noticed Miss Brown, and the sight would cover him with confusion. He would mutter an apology, hastily seize the cuffs, and withdraw. This happened time and time again — the situation on each occasion repeating itself exactly — and every time I was equally embarrassed for my father.

I have talked about the development of my literary ambitions which I associate with the summer of 1927 and the solitary walking and brooding that I indulged in at that time. I remember one Monday evening about this time, after I had been playing for Miss Brown a piece by Frank Bridge whose name I forget but whose opening cadences I can still remember: I liked the piece, and played it well, and the music was running through my head as I leaned out of my bedroom window and listened to the sounds of Edinburgh coming up from the street below — housewives beating carpets in the back greens of Livingstone Place, boys playing cricket in the Meadows, and the distant sound of bagpipes from the East Meadows, where public concerts were provided by the Corporation. Gradually the strains of the distant pipe music ousted the piano music from my consciousness, and I listened, unspeakably moved. I found the sound of bagpipes deeply moving; it awakened my sense of Scottish history with its violence and its pageantry and its fatal predilection for the lost cause. As I grew up Scotland became for me more and more an emotion rather than a country, and I would surrender myself to the emotion with a pleasing melancholy.

But of course I was Jewish, and my ancestors had no part in this romantic history: theirs had been a darker and more glorious destiny. My pride in Jewish history and my feeling for its particular kind of sadness existed side by side with my attitude to Scotland. It was largely a matter of mood (how much, in my childhood, was largely a matter of mood!). The Scottish mood rose to the sound of the bagpipes or the sight of Edinburgh Castle fading in the purple darkness; the Jewish mood came with the elegiac synagogue chants and the plaintive melodies of Jewish liturgy and folksong. Each mood excluded the other: in the Scottish mood the Jewish world seemed distant and unimportant, and in the Jewish mood Scottish history and traditions seemed modern and shabby. It was now that I became acutely aware of living in two worlds, or rather of moving freely between one and the other. Bagpipe music and synagogue melody represented the two poles between which my sensibility moved. I accepted this dualism as part of the nature of things, and looking back now I wonder at the ease with which I did so.

My last year at school — 1929 to 1930 — was my happiest and most fruitful. Having passed my Higher Leaving Certificate the year before in all the necessary subjects, including Mathematics, Physics and Chemistry, I was now free to drop the subjects in which I was less interested and less able, and concentrate on English, History, Latin and Greek. This year was a kind of interregnum between school and university, with something of the best points of each. The classes were small and the subjects were congenial. One got to know the masters, who appeared at last as helpful human beings rather than merely as teachers. I worked hard, writing extra Latin proses because the Latin master had interested me in the possibility of imitating different kinds of Latin prose style. I read an immense amount outside the regular school work, taking out from the Carnegie Library the works of Ibsen and Strindberg and Bjornson as well as Galsworthy, Shaw and Conrad; I read — and resented — Spengler's *Decline of the West*; I took the poems of Keats and Spenser with me on walks to Blackford Hill; I rolled Homer's Greek on my tongue and thought with pity and almost with contempt of those who were unable to do likewise. I even, in a very small way, became a leader in a school activity, for I played the violin in the school orchestra and was now made its leader. I contributed to the *Watsonian* a verse translation of a chorus from Euripides' *Medea* and of a poem by Alfred de Vigny. And at the end of a year pulsing with literary ambition and self-confidence I won a scholarship to the university and enough prizes to satisfy even my view of what my father would wish for me. On prizegiving day, as I staggered off the platform balancing some £20 worth of books (representing special prizes in English, Latin, Greek, History and essay writing), I thought of my father sitting among the parents and being at last really proud of his son. He shook hands with me afterwards and said 'Well done!' — something he had never done before, for he was a shy man who could not easily speak words of praise to those close to him. Later, at the woodwork exhibition held in the school's art room, I watched him manoeuvre his way into the vicinity of the headmaster and his deputy and overheard him thanking them, in a courtly little speech, for all they had done for me. As a matter of fact, neither of those particular individuals had done anything for me; but they stood for those who had, and my father's act was symbolic. It set a seal on my school career. I looked across at my father and was proud of his pride in me; I felt that I had done something, had helped to increase his dignity and vindicate the character of the Jew in Scotland. I had not let him down. Walking home across the Meadows with my parents, carrying my heavy load of prize books, I felt that I had no more to ask of life. The July sun was shining; ahead lay the summer holidays; and in the Autumn the university and the promise of the free life of letters.

CHAPTER FOUR

I believe a schoolteacher wrote a book some years ago with the title *Friday Thank God*. That phrase expresses perfectly my attitude to the arrival of the weekend during term time when I was a schoolboy. The daily grind of school, with its abundant homework, its fierce competition, the sense of never being able to relax, pressed heavily upon me, in spite of the fact that I often enjoyed the actual class-room work. Waking up in the morning with the knowledge that one simply had to get out of bed, that there was no possibility of turning over for an extra doze, and seeing the hours of school stretching ahead, was a dismal experience, especially on a Monday. We had a maid once who would climb each morning with grim steps up to the attic floor where Lionel and I slept in one bedroom and my sister Sylvia in another, and announce in deep, funereal tones: 'Lionel, David, Sylvia — time!' I used to lie waiting for that ominous tread on the uncarpeted attic stairs (they were covered with a flower-patterned yellow linoleum), and the voice it heralded sounded in my ears like a summons to damnation. The anticipation was always worse than the reality; I don't remember ever being especially unhappy in class; but the oppressive weight of the knowledge of a full day's school ahead remained a characteristic sensation of my childhood and disappeared only after I had left school and entered the university, where the smaller number of classes to be attended and the freedom of the student to come and go meant a completely new kind of academic world. To wake up on a Thursday morning was to feel the end of the week already lying ahead, and Friday morning was positively rose-coloured. The last 'period' (as each of our lessons was called) on a Friday, whatever the subject, had its special happy flavour of the end of the week, and one walked home from school on a Friday afternoon (however much homework had been assigned for the Monday) with the tread of an escaped prisoner. Friday night, with two solid days before school again, was the best night of the week; Saturday night, with still a whole day between it and Monday, was pleasant in a quite different way; Sunday night was full of the threat of Monday morning.

Sometimes there were unexpected respites — a half holiday to let us attend a football match which some unforeseen circumstance had caused to be cancelled the preceding Saturday, or the sudden dismissal of school an hour or two before the usual time because of some unexpected crisis or celebration. But these were few and far between. Once a term we had the annual mid-term holiday, a Monday off, which made a luxuriously long weekend (but it seemed to go just as fast as ordinary weekends), and occasionally in winter if there had been a continuous hard frost for some days we would get a whole day's 'skating holiday'. These were blessed breaks in routine, but not, of course, comparable to the holidays we got at Christmas and at Easter — three weeks each in my earlier school days, later tragically reduced to a fortnight and then (if my recollection of loss is not misleading me) to a mere ten days. But 'the' holidays were the summer holidays, the two months' vacation we got in the summer time, and it was these months towards which the whole year moved.

There were three phases of the summer holidays. First the week or two at the end of the summer term, when the year's marks were already in (so that nothing that one did *counted*) yet classes still went on. There was a wonderful sense of relaxation about those days. The unrelenting competition in marks which had gone on throughout the school year suddenly ceased, for the prizes and scholarships were now allotted; masters unbent, and not only amused us with Latin crosswords or intriguing stunts in the science laboratories, but would chat in human and friendly fashion about climbing and fishing. I remember once, at this time of the year, 'Billie' Williams, our Mathematics master, sat down unexpectedly on the bench beside me and began to give me advice on trout fishing, going into such practical details as the price of rods and telling me where I could get a cheap but serviceable one. This period between the end of the examinations and the prizegiving (with which the school session formally concluded) was in some respects the best part of all the year, for the other two parts of summer were lying happily ahead — the month at the seaside, and the further month of freedom in Edinburgh before school started again. Pure bliss seemed to stretch endlessly on the horizon. Two months seemed a long, long time in those days; indeed, I used to have the feeling that for all practical purposes I could look forward to a period of permanent felicity. I would walk home across the Meadows in the July sunshine, wearing my summer school clothes of grey cricket shirt, grey shorts, and red Watson's blazer, and savour my happiness with conscious relish. I could hardly believe that three strenuous school terms had indeed rolled away and the longed for, dreamed of, almost (it seemed at times) mythical summer holidays were at hand, unspoilt as yet, lying intact and promising just ahead. It all seemed too good to be true. Wishes didn't come true in this life — I knew that: all my early childhood I longed desperately for a tricycle, which my parents could never afford, and later the wish was transferred to a bicycle, and there, too, I was permanently disappointed. (I bought my first bicycle for myself when I was twenty-one, with prize money I had won at Edinburgh University.) How often had I stood outside sweet shops with empty pockets longing for a penny or two to materialise somehow or hung on the outskirts of a crowd around an ice-cream barrow wondering whether the ice-cream man would be miraculously inspired to offer me a 'cornet' or a 'slider' free. These things never happened. (The few pence a week pocket money we received was to be put into a money-box and saved, and during our early childhood Lionel, Sylvia and I never had anything to spend for ourselves.) Yet summer and the summer holidays did come; the school year did come to an end; and one did find oneself at last standing by the trunks and suitcases outside No.6, Millerfield Place, waiting for the taxi (glorious vehicle) that was to convey the family and its luggage to the railway station.

It had been horse cabs when I was very young, but the taxi soon established itself in my gallery of exciting and anticipated objects, and the very smell of its exhaust set the heart beating faster. The leathery smell inside, the straps hanging down from the adjustable, rattling windows, the little folding seats that could be pulled out for us children to sit on — how thoroughly delectable these things were! And then to watch as the taxi came into the precincts of the station, marked by the appearance of hoardings covered with advertising posters — Stephen's ink, Oxo, Bovril, Virol ('growing girls need it'), Pear's soap, the Pickwick, the Owl and the Waverley pen, that come as a Boon and a Blessing to men. These were signposts to adventure, indications that we were nearing the actual station, with its infinite glories. People have complained of the typical British railway station, with its noise, its dirt, its apparent confusion; but as a child I found it magnificently thrilling (an attitude I have never wholly lost). Porters rushing about with barrows heaped with luggage, the noise of trains arriving and departing, carriage doors slamming, the guard blowing his whistle, engines letting off steam, uniformed boys with trays strapped to their chests shouting 'Chocolates! Cigarettes!', trolleys with newspapers and confectionary being wheeled along the platform, everywhere the sense of movement, bustle, excitement and romance. And to know that one was going off oneself in a train, out beyond Haymarket tunnel, across the Forth Bridge, beyond, beyond — such knowledge made the railway station the most perfect spot on earth. Waverley Station, Edinburgh, was an especially good station; it was large, busy, noisy, with a great number of platforms and trains departing for almost every possible direction.

On these occasions my father always wore an air of business-like efficiency. I had watched him write out and tie on the labels, heard him ring up for the taxi, observed his supervision of the taxi-driver as he stowed the luggage in the taxi (always a difficult job, for our family travelled with mountains of luggage), accompanied him to one of the station bookstalls where he methodically bought papers to read in the train — a *Scotsman* for himself, a *Bulletin*, perhaps, for my mother, and a *Children's Newspaper* or sometimes even (for we were on holiday) an illustrated magazine or two for us children. And now as he collected his family round him at the barrier and presented the tickets, he was very much the paterfamilias leading a family expedition. He would personally see that the heavy luggage was safely stowed in the luggage van, waving his stick at porters and directing them in tones of firm authority that only occasionally gave way to accents of urgency and even anxiety. But at last we were settled in the compartment, the hand luggage stowed safely on the luggage rack, the corner seats argued over and finally allocated — there being five of us and a compartment, of course, having only four corners. The atmosphere of tension and hurry which had surrounded all our movements suddenly relaxed; we were early after all; and there was plenty of time before the train moved off.

Sitting in the train, waiting for the guard's whistle to announce to the engine driver that it was time for him to start, I would revel in anticipation. And when the train began slowly to move, passing the porters and their barrows as they stood on the platform, passing the bookstall, the advertisements on the wall, moving out into the open past the hissing engines of stationary trains, the real adventure began. Through the deep cutting that traversed Princes Street Gardens at the base of the Castle Rock, then into the dark of Haymarket tunnel, a brief stop at Haymarket station, and out past the western suburbs of Edinburgh to the open fields that lay between the city and South Queensferry, where the Forth Bridge began. As the train rumbled across the Forth Bridge we three children all crowded to the window to look down on the Forth lying like a river on a map hundreds of feet below. The water lapping the shores, the ships looking like toys yet at the same time excitingly real, the whole sense of living geography that came over me as I looked down from the moving train, made me feel strangely as though I were both viewing and participating in the grand rolling of the earth in its relentless diurnal movement. I felt curiously moved. Years later, I discovered that precisely this emotion was brought back on reading the lines of Keats:

The moving waters at their priestlike task
Of pure ablution round earth's human shores.

It was something to do with a sense of the steady way in which the world of geography carried on unperturbed by the petty daily affairs of men in cities, and I recaptured it vividly not long ago when watching the waves break on a deserted beach at night.

In 1920 we spent August in Kilrenny, a tiny village a mile away from the Fife fishing town of Anstruther. This was the first of many holidays spent on the shores of Fife — at St Andrews, at Leven (twice), and for seven successive years at Crail. But the 1920 holiday was especially exciting, for it was the first time the family had gone off for a month's holiday since we had settled in Edinburgh in March 1919. In 1919 because of my mother's illness and presumably also because the move to Edinburgh had meant enough travel (and expense) for one year, we did not go away at all. In earlier years we had spent our holidays either with my paternal grandparents in Leeds or with my mother's people in Liverpool. This time we were going away to the seaside, like so many other middle-class people, and my joy in the adventure was increased by the knowledge that we were behaving as a family should.

The house we were bound for was one of a group of three which stood together at the edge of a common and which, apart from a few farm houses and a cottage or two, constituted the entire village of Kilrenny. My father had learned of it through an advertisement in the Edinburgh daily paper, *The Scotsman*. The description of the house in the advertisement had sounded suitable, and the rent was reasonable, so my father wrote off to the owner (an elderly spinster by the name of Miss Gardner) to ask for further particulars. Miss Gardner's reply arrived one afternoon in July, soon after I had come home from school. I was lying lazily on the dining-room sofa, and mother was sitting in an armchair in a corner of the room, when my father entered with a letter in his hand. I remember him standing in the recess by the bay window reading out the letter to my mother. As he read, it dawned upon me that this was a description of the house where we might be going for our holidays, and I listened intently. I have a vivid recollection of my father reading out, in a somewhat sing-song tone, the phrase '. . . and it has a W.C. . . .', emphasising rhythmically the first, third and fifth syllables, and giving an approving nod of his head. I knew at that moment that he would take the house. And I said to myself: '*As long as I live, I shall never forget Daddy standing there by the window reading out those words*: "*and it has a* W.C.."'

Having crossed the Forth Bridge, the train wound up the Fife coast, every now and again coming right out onto the sea, running by villages, harbours, golf courses, beaches, stretches of rocks and shingle. One caught fascinating glimpses of a calm sea rippling up a sandy cove, a patch of seaweed covered rocks, children playing on a beach, a golfer bending down to put his ball on the tee. Aberdour; Burntisland, where one caught a glimpse of fairly large freight vessels in the harbour; a stretch of bright red sand which seemed to be a deposit from an aluminium factory (this is what I believed as a child; I have not the remotest idea whether this is the true explanation of the red sand or indeed of what an aluminium factory is); Kirkcaldy, where the smell of linoleum floated strongly in, from the factories of Barrie, Ostlere and Shepherd; Dysart; Thornton Junction, where the line swerved inland; back to the coast again at Leven; a brief stop at the tiny station of Lundin Links; the picturesque fishing villages and holiday resorts of Largo, Elie, St Monans and Pittenweem; and finally

Anstruther, the nearest station to Kilrenny. Miss Gardner had arranged to have a car meet us, and we bundled in and were driven to the house. It had that half musty, cottagey smell that all country houses seem to have, and I took that as a guarantee of its authenticity, proof that we were well away from the city. It was, in fact, a thrilling smell. I discovered that I was to share an attic bedroom with my brother Lionel. The evening light was coming in at the window when I first saw it, and it looked golden and old-fashioned and rustic and peaceful.

Lionel, Sylvia and I were up early the next morning, and we had explored the common before breakfast. There was a burn running through it, which was very satisfactory; there were also some local small boys who shouted derisive remarks at us, which was less pleasing. After breakfast, mother chased us all (including my father) out of the house, while she unpacked. My father decided that we ought to find out the way to the sea. He appeared dressed for the expedition. He had discarded the black frock-coat he wore almost always in Edinburgh (except on very hot days, when he would wear, at home, a black alpaca jacket) and wore instead a dark grey lounge suit. He still wore his black bow tie and his stiff collar, but the stiff artificial shirt front was gone, and so were the stiff cuffs. On his head he had neither the glossy silk hat he wore in Edinburgh on all occasions of even the slightest formality, nor the broad-brimmed black soft hat he used in the city while out on more ordinary business, but a cloth 'travelling cap' of a brownish-grey colour. He wore a dark grey topcoat and carried a stout walking stick. On future holidays his old-fashioned formality of attire was to diminish much further, under the pressure of his children's criticism and a general change in the atmosphere of the times; in Crail in the early 1930s he wore a blue blazer and grey flannel trousers with a grey sweater and a cricket shirt with a light grey tie; but in 1920 he had not yet learned to relax so completely. Earnest idealist that he was, he felt it necessary to carry around with him, even on holiday, some indication of his responsibilities as representative of and spokesman for the Jewish way of life before the clergy and laity of Scotland. He was forty years old then.

We discovered that it was quite a long walk to the sea, and to get to the shingly beach we had to pass through the adjacent village of Cellardyke. It astonished us that in less than a mile we should have moved from one village to another, but it added to the sense of adventure and exploration. At Cellardyke we found a small grocer's and confectioner's shop, and my father, announcing that he would buy some sweets, marshalled us all in. He inquired of the proprietor (Mr Allan, I think his name was) with grave courtesy what kind of chocolates he had in stock, and Mr Allan brought out samples of different kinds and laid them on the counter. 'Very good these,' he said, of one variety. 'Try one.' And to our astonishment he popped one briskly into my father's mouth. My father chewed the chocolate meditatively, then nodded, and, with an almost ritual solemnity, proceeded to purchase half a pound. Mr Allan then directed us to the beach, where we spent the rest of the morning.

Spending a considerable part of every day by the beach was a ritual with us when on holiday. We came for the sea air, and nothing was going to prevent us from getting it. I don't remember bad weather ever keeping us indoors: rain or shine we were in the fresh air absorbing health. My father in particular would waste no second of his precious holiday. I have known him sit outside for hours in the pouring rain, holding an umbrella over his head as he gazed meditatively out to sea. At the end of the month, sun, wind and rain had always weathered his face to a rich brown, and when the Jewish High Festivals came, as they often did, early in September, my father's weather-beaten face would look quite startling as he stood in the pulpit in his white *kittel*.

My mother got out less often; she had the house to run, and she was left to cook the meals and wash the dishes while the rest of the family sought the open air. Sometimes we had a maid with us on holiday, sometimes we hadn't, but in either case my mother had much to do in the house, and never really had a proper holiday. She would join us at the beach after we had been there for an hour or two, and leave early to prepare the next meal. She did go bathing with us however (sea-bathing was another daily ritual in our family when on holiday) and it was she who taught us all to swim, including my father. Heroically determined, he learned to swim at the age of forty, and though he never swam well, he swam conscientiously, and always stayed in the water much longer than any of the rest of us. His technique of bathing was all his own. He would walk into the sea up to his waist, and then bob right down until the sea covered his head, two or three times in rapid succession. Then he would act as though he were washing his face with sea water. And after that he would swim a short distance with short, rapid strokes, before standing up and repeating the ducking performance. Mother would swim gracefully about for a while and then take each of us children out to deepish water and, holding us up by the chin, give us a swimming lesson. Then she would warm herself up by a further swim before coming out. I may be wrong, but my impression is that my father wore the same bathing costume (our family always stuck to that good old Victorian term) all the years I knew him; it started off by being a very dark blue, but after some years it became a faded light blue in colour and also got pretty tattered and frayed about the edges. Some time about 1930 my mother bought him a rainbow-coloured beach-robe, of which he grew very fond. He would wear it down to the water's edge, where he would discard it while he went into the water, and then put it on as soon as he came out. I can see him now, panting and dripping, with the water streaming down his greying hair, as he struggles into his rainbow robe.

Swimming was not the only sport that my father took up relatively late in life. In 1922 we spent our summer holiday in Leven, a Fife town of some respectable size, beside the coal port of Methil. Leven, though far from being as quiet and rustic as Kilrenny, had a large and excellent beach and it also had several first-rate golfcourses. It was here, on the comparatively easy 'ladies' course', that Lionel and I first played golf, and it was here, too, that my father first played the royal and ancient game. The three of us started off with three clubs between us — a driver, a cleek, and a putter — and no instruction of any kind. We simply imitated what we deemed to be the movements of other golfers. My father, who was a small man of robust physique but with relatively poor physical co-ordination, would address the ball with a swift, desperate, jerking movement; it never occurred to him that he might have a better chance of hitting it if he took a slow back swing. After pondering the ball for a moment he would jerk his club back a few feet and then, without any pause at all, jerk it forward to the ball. He would miss, or top or slice the ball more often than not, but sometimes, by sheer good luck, would land it a smart crack which would send it a fair distance. His gratification at such a lucky shot was immense. I believe he thought that all success in such physical activities was due entirely to good luck, and he had no awareness of how impossibly bad his golf was. He had the hands of a writer and scholar, with stubby fingers which looked most at home when curved about a pen. He was quite handy about the house in such things as mending fuses, and he fancied himself as a watchmaker and would pick away at a broken watch with a pin until he had rendered it beyond repair, but he was hopeless at anything that required delicacy of physical co-ordination. He was occasionally taken out fishing by a wealthy member of his congregation who had taken up the sports of the landed gentry, and on one occasion he caught the back of his coat with his very first cast. He was regarded as dangerous with a fishing rod, but not to the fish. He had great stamina, however, and until fairly late in life would walk for miles without fatigue.

My father, Lionel and I playing golf together was, I suppose, something of a symbol of the attitude of the Daiches family to sport. With one set of three clubs between the three of us, we would pass the clubs around as needed, often to the amazement and sometimes to the annoyance of

golfers coming up behind us. Often I would dash fifty yards
to where my father was, to hand him the cleek after I had
used it myself, while Lionel, who could not be bothered to
go and fetch it after my father had used it, would make his
slow progress down the fairway with a putter. We would
lose balls frequently too; my father's propensity to wild
slicing often resulting in the disappearance of the ball into
a clump of whin bushes after his drive. Once we played with
one ball as well as only three clubs between the three of us,
taking alternate shots. This was at the very beginning of our
golfing careers. The next year we acquired a mashie and a
jigger, and a little later my father discovered that a putting
green was really more his style. He became fairly efficient
as a putter, and would often invite Lionel or myself to what
he called 'a game of putt'. Lionel and I continued to play,
on the Balcomie Golf Course at Crail, with one set of clubs
between us. Eventually Lionel gave up golf altogether and
I inherited the five family clubs, two of which I replaced
with new ones bought at Thornton's, in Edinburgh, with
bursary money. I played occasionally with schoolmates on
the Braid Hills course, and continued to play sporadically
during my university days. I was never very good, but did
acquire a modest competence at the game. I never had more
than six clubs, and gave up the game completely when it
became the fashion for golfers to carry a whole armoury
of weapons around with them on the golf course. When
I see golfers today going off to play with their enormous
array of clubs, I think of the old men of Edinburgh in the
1920s who would go round the ancient and modest little
course at Bruntsfield with a single club and then walk slowly
home in the summer dusk, with the club held horizontally
by the middle of the shaft, swinging to and fro as the arms
swung.

I think it was on our summer holidays in Fife that my father
first learned to relax. His earlier life had been intellectually
strenuous, intense, dedicated. To become, over a period
of a few years, at the same time an authority on David
Hume and an orthodox rabbi thoroughly grounded in the

enormous complexities of Talmudic theory and practice was a remarkable feat, and can have left no time for relaxation of any kind. And then, as a young minister in Hull and later in Sunderland, fired with the passionate ideal of a living Judaism domiciled happily in an English cultural context, preaching, lecturing, exhorting, pleading, before apathetic audiences in shabby synagogues and meeting places, belligerently optimistic, positively messianic in his visionary hopes yet grimly realistic in his appraisal of the material he had to work with — it was an exhausting life, with no room anywhere for triviality. When he settled in Edinburgh in March, 1919, to become rabbi of the Edinburgh Hebrew Congregation and virtual spiritual head of the Jews in Scotland, he soon made emotional contact, as it were, with eighteenth-century Edinburgh (he was already familiar with it intellectually) and developed a Scottish-Jewish ideal that increased its hold on him with the years. And it was on his seaside holidays in Scotland that he learned to relax.

It did not happen all at once. Each year he shed more of his formal clothing when on holiday and became more successful in temporarily laying aside his official personality. At Crail in the late 1920s and early 1930s the process went on apace, and when, after my final year at Edinburgh University, the family went to the north-west Highlands for August, my father had acquired (but of course for holiday use only) something of the air and apparel of a sporting country gentleman. And while in earlier years he had taken away with him for holiday reading some heavy philosophical or theological volume, I once found him in the summer of 1934 reading a paperbound French novel. His smoking habits changed too, and this affected more than his holiday practice. My father was a connoisseur of Havana cigars, and for years would smoke nothing else — which meant that he often smoked nothing at all, for he could not afford to buy many Havana cigars and depended largely on presents of cigars he received occasionally from more well-to-do members of his congregation (who were, incidentally, few in number: the Jews of Edinburgh in those days were not on the whole a prosperous lot). He would save a few Havana cigars to smoke on his holiday. But once — it was at Leven, I think, in 1922 — not having any Havana cigars and not being able to afford to buy any, he decided to try cigarettes for the first time in his life — not ordinary cigarettes, of course, but Russian cigarettes, which somehow had more dignity than the vulgar variety and at the same time tasted perhaps a little more like a Havana cigar. But they were unsatisfactory. My father puffed at them in the clumsy way in which a cigar smoker will smoke a cigarette, and he was manifestly unsatisfied. For the next few years it was again Havana cigars or nothing. And then, about 1930, he was persuaded to try a pipe as a holiday smoke. A member of his congregation presented him with a curved-stem pipe and half a pound of Balkan Sobranie, the richest and most cigar-like of tobaccos. From that time on, he was a regular pipe smoker, always smoking Balkan Sobranie tobacco and always using a pipe with a curved stem. Of course, he still smoked Havana cigars when he could get them, but during the day, not only on holiday but also at home when he sat working in his study, he would puff away at his pipe. He was not a skilful pipe-smoker, and he would allow moisture to accumulate in his pipe so that his puffing often produced an audible bubbling. I remember once, when Lionel and I were in our early twenties and had been for some years pipe smokers ourselves, finding one of our father's pipes on the dining-room mantelpiece and discovering that it had become so carbonised that the hollow in the bowl was only about a quarter of an inch in diameter. Much amused, we pointed this out to our father, who smiled shyly and said that he had noticed that the pipe seemed to have been getting smaller but he had never been quite sure why. Either Lionel or I — I cannot remember which of us, now — scraped out the bowl for him and he received the restored pipe with gratitude and delight.

We first went to Crail in 1927, and went there for seven successive summers, generally, though not always, to the

same house. This little Fife town thus takes a special place
in my recollection of childhood summers. It was — and
is — an unpretentious but picturesque town on the sea
almost at the eastern extremity of Fife, the East Neuk of
Fife as it is called. There was an old stone harbour at one
end of the town, a pleasant but small beach at the other,
and a great variety of rocks and rockpools between. Our
time would be divided between the beach, from which
we bathed daily (except Saturdays) and the rocks, where
Lionel and I would spend hour after hour watching the
marine life and catching the 'grannies' and other fish that
inhabited the pools. Sometimes we would go for walks to
Anstruther, four miles away, or to St Andrews, ten miles
in the opposite direction, or, more frequently, to the big
beach at Balcomie, round at the other side of Fife Ness,
where the sand was lighter and finer than the sand at Crail.
There was a confectioner's, known as Mrs Aird's, where
the young people would gather of an evening to buy ice
cream or fish and chips, but our family was seldom there.
True, we all had an ice cream a day, after bathing: that
was a ritual, and the ice cream was bought from a stand
by the beach. (It strikes me with amazement now that we
should have wanted to eat ice cream after bathing in the
chill waters of the North Sea.) But, quite apart from the
fact that Mrs Aird's fish and chips would not have been
kosher, having been fried in animal fat, we did not mingle
with the 'fast' set that frequented such haunts: our holiday
was open-air and active and innocent. We swam, walked,
fished, played on the sand, occasionally played golf on the
Balcomie golf course, or sat reading by the sea. Towards
the end of August, as the evenings began to draw in, we
would walk in the dusk along the Castle Walk, a picturesque
path which began round the corner from our house and ran
along the top of a field which sloped down to the rocks and
the sea. There were wooden benches placed at intervals
along the Castle Walk, and there my father would often
sit in wet weather or in the evening after dark. He made
friends with a Mr Greig, Church of Scotland minister from

Airdrie, and they would sit side by side at night talking of the differences and similarities between their two religions while the fragrant aroma of Balkan Sobranie floated over the Castle Walk. Walking along there after dark, I could smell the tobacco and hear the murmur of voices before I could make out the figures on the bench, and the tobacco smell and the murmur of voices mingled with the splash of the sea below to produce a complex sensation which I still recall vividly to bring back my father in Crail in late August.

But Mrs Aird's remained a disturbing and even a seductive image. These were the years of my adolescence, and the young men and women hanging around Mrs Aird's stood for a world of sexual adventure whose very thought was absolutely incompatible with the atmosphere of our family life. As far as Lionel and I were able to discover, sex did not exist in the Daiches family. Neither of our parents ever addressed to us a single word about it, at any time. My father's notion, I think, was that one kept oneself pure by hard work and idealistic ambitions until one had completed one's professional training, and then a suitable bride was brought to one's attention, with whom one fell in love and in marriage to whom one's sex interests were first awakened. I found my own adolescence disturbing and embarrassing, and I thought the imaginations to which it gave rise were both unique and guilty. I suppose it is comic or even pathetic that a small confectioner's-cum-fish and chip shop in a little seaside town should have represented to me, and I think to Lionel as well, a world of forbidden desire. For years afterwards the smell of fish and chips had a more erotic tang to me than perfumes named 'Ecstasy' or 'Desire', though by the time I was really grown up my taste had become more conventional in this respect.

August always went by too quickly, and all too soon we would find ourselves preparing for the return to Edinburgh. Preparations began a day or two before we actually left. There was an immense amount of packing to be done, which Mother undertook pretty well single-handed. For years we travelled with our own meat dishes (for we could not eat off the meat dishes of a non-Jewish house) and Mother had supplies of meat sent out by post from the Edinburgh Jewish butcher. Packing a trunk full of dishes was an arduous business, and eventually Mother gave it up and we went vegetarian throughout August — which was no hardship, for Mother could do marvellous things with fish (the term vegetarian in our family meant simply eating no meat but did not exclude fish). Slowly and gradually, and I am sure never consciously on my parents' part, we relaxed a bit in the matter of diet. When she was first married Mother baked all her own bread, but ceased to do this after her illness in 1919. And on holiday one found oneself going a little further than one would have done in the city. In Edinburgh, we usually ate bread from the Jewish bakery, but occasionally we would get a loaf from a non-Jewish shop. Cakes and biscuits we regularly got from non-Jewish sources. But though Mother would buy ordinary cakes from a non-Jewish baker, she would always make her own pastry, for pastry from a gentile shop was liable to have been made with lard. On holiday, however, pastries started to creep in among the cakes bought for tea, and nobody raised the question of what they were made with. 'Squashed flies' — cakes made by squashing a mass of currants between two layers of pastry — were originally forbidden if not home-made, but squashed flies from an ordinary baker first found their way to our table when we were on holiday in St Andrews. True, we never bathed on Saturdays or did anything on that day except sit and read on the beach or go for decorous walks; and we said our daily Hebrew prayers and read the weekly portion of the law in Crail as in Edinburgh; yet the strictness of religious observance was relaxed when we were away on holiday, slightly and by slow degrees, but definitely.

I have mentioned that my father unbent on holiday in a way he rarely did at home. During the last few years that the whole family took its holiday together — when I was a student at Edinburgh and a research student at Oxford — I was able, on holiday walks, to speak to him in a man-to-man way for the first time in my life. We had of course often argued together in a friendly way, but never really talked as though we were contemporaries and equals. But now he began to talk to Lionel and myself as though he really wanted our opinion. He would even ask our advice on something he was writing or some course of action he was contemplating. By this time he had become very much part of the Scottish scene, a Scottish rabbi with the emphasis as much on the 'Scottish' as on the 'rabbi', devoted to the Scottish countryside, more and more regarding his Judaism as part of the Scottish milieu. I have a clear picture of him one Saturday morning in August 1934, in a remote West Highland village, sitting on a rock looking out at the Hebrides, his old dogeared *Chumesh* (Hebrew Pentateuch) open on his lap at that day's portion of the law. His head was covered, of course, because he was reading the Bible; but it was with a soft-brimmed hat, not a skull-cap. And I remember the evening of the same day: we had stood on the shore watching the western sun go down with unusual splendour, and as we lingered there in the hushed Highland night I heard my father singing faintly to himself the old Hebrew song about Elijah the prophet returning to his people, one of the songs traditionally sung after the Sabbath had departed and comfort was required to face the workaday world again.

It was on this holiday, too, that we took an excursion on one of the MacBrayne steamers to the Isle of Skye. The weather was dull, and rain threatened; Lionel and I slipped down to the ship's bar for a comfortable beer. We were seated in a corner drinking export ale when we both became aware simultaneously of our father sitting at the opposite corner of the bar with a glass of lager before him. I had never known him enter a bar before, and never known him drink beer, though he had done so, I knew, in his student days. He took his glass and came over to our table. 'Hello,' he said, 'What are you doing here?' We laughed, and replied: 'Same as you.' He smiled, and seemed at a loss for words — shy but not embarrassed. Finally, he said:

'It's a funny thing: your beer is dark brown and mine is pale yellow.'

That was in 1934. When I look back on holidays by the sea, however, it is my childhood in the twenties that I recall most frequently. Just as I remember so vividly the joy and excitement of setting out on holiday, so I remember the desperate desire to cling to the last moments before time had ticked them away and we had to leave for home. I used to stand on the beach and look around and say to myself: 'I'm here now, at *this minute*, and nothing can take this minute way.' But it went. Coming home from the holidays had its compensations, however. There was the train journey again, and train journeys were always exciting, in whatever direction one was going. And there were always things of our own that we had perforce left behind which we were glad to get back to. School was almost a month away still. As the evenings drew in and the return of school grew close, the idea of winter grew attractively cosy. School itself — a new year, a new class, new books — had its attractive side, and I would promise myself that this year I would really master everything from the very first, never leave things to be swotted up in a rush before the exams but by steady work achieve an effortless mastery of every subject and end the year covered with scholarships and prizes and glory. This resolution generally lasted about a week after the opening of term, but it was wonderfully sustaining while it did last.

How large our house in Millerfield Place looked when we first came back to it after our holiday! How high the ceilings were, yet how shut-in the house was, with other houses staring at us from across the street. 'Yesterday at this time I was swimming in the sea;' 'a week ago today we went for a walk to St Andrews.' Slowly we ceased to dwell on our past holiday and surrendered to the different excitement of Autumn. There was a briskness in the September air that moved one's thoughts to the future. My father had resumed his frock-coat and formality of manner and was busy preparing for the High Festivals. How right, I used to feel, was the Jewish tradition of having the New Year in September! Everything was beginning afresh, a new working year was setting in, a chance to do bigger and better things than ever before. The year began with the retreat from out of doors, with the drawing of curtains and the poking up of the fire, the re-establishment of the claims of the domestic interior. In the gardens of the quiet streets of South Edinburgh they were burning dead leaves, and the smell of the burning leaves was for me the sad-sweet dirge of the outdoor life, of the life of sand and sea and field, and at the same time the heady promise of — of what? Of something better, anyway, something exciting, something really worth while, something I could achieve myself by an effort of the will. Yes, I could and would: this year I would show them!

CHAPTER FIVE

I always found it next to impossible to imagine my father as a child. This was not only because, as a rabbi and a well-known public figure in Edinburgh, he had a dignity and formality of manner infinitely removed from the world of childhood, but also because I knew nothing of the circumstances of his childhood and thus found it impossible to visualise them. I am not even sure where or when he was born. The date of his birth he usually gave as 1880, but his birth certificate was dated 10 March, 1881. He had some story of the records of the town in Lithuania where he was born having been destroyed by fire and new birth certificates issued later to replace those which had been burned: the issuing clerk evidently drew on his memory for the details, and got the date of my father's birth wrong by a year. My father himself seemed somewhat vague about the story; but he always maintained that his true date of birth was 1880, in spite of his birth certificate. His insurance company, however, insisted on believing the birth certificate, and that was to his advantage as far as life insurance premiums were concerned. Exactly where in Poland he was born I am not certain but I believe he was born in Vilna, though he spent his early childhood in Neustadt-Scherwindt, by the Lithuanian–German border. I am sure that my father talked as though Poland, not Lithuania, were the country of his birth, and I believe that Vilna was Polish for part of its history; but my relatives assure me that it should be considered Lithuanian. Both Poland and Lithuania were then, of course, under Russian rule.

One of the reasons for my vagueness about these details

is that my father disliked talking about them. I don't think he made more than half a dozen references to his childhood during all the years that I knew him. He was the second son of a distinguished rabbi and scholar, and scion of a long line of rabbis and scholars which stretched back to the early Middle Ages. From all I can gather, his infancy was spent in strenuous Jewish and Hebrew scholarship: I remember he once referred to his studying Talmud as a small boy by the light of rush candles stuck in the wall. This suggests poverty as well as precocity, yet I don't think the family were poor, for I understand that my grandmother brought with her a very respectable dowry and for some time her father supported my grandfather while he lived a life of pure scholarship and meditation. My father once told a story of a 'nurse' putting her head out of the window and shrieking out that a pig had got into the courtyard, to which he (then a very small boy) impertinently replied that he had seen no pig before the nurse appeared at the window. A nurse and a courtyard suggest some degree of prosperity. However that may be, my grandfather sent his sons to high school across the German border, in Koenigsberg, where my father attended the *Gymnasium* and acquired a sound education in the Classics. The only other fact I remember hearing about my father's childhood is that his parents did not make a party for him at the celebration of his *barmitzvah* (confirmation, at the age of thirteen), as is the usual custom: the reason for this was that his elder brother, my Uncle Samuel, had made himself so sick with overeating at the party held in celebration of *his* barmitzvah that my grandparents thought it safer to omit that part of the proceedings when my father's turn came. My Uncle Samuel — who became a biblical scholar of international reputation — remained extremely fat throughout his adult life: and I still cannot help associating his fatness with that *barmitzvah* party at which he blocked my father's chances of a party by gorging himself.

From the *Gymnasium* at Koenigsberg my father went to Berlin University to study philosophy under Paulsen and at the same time to prosecute his rabbinical studies at the Hildesheimer Seminary, a Jewish theological college which had as its ideal the combination of strict Jewish orthodoxy and sound training in traditional rabbinics with a knowledge and appreciation of secular western culture. The Hildesheimer ideal burned brightly in my father all his life, being eventually transformed by him into his unique Scottish–Jewish synthesis. From Berlin he went to Leipzig, where he eventually graduated A.M., ph.D. with a thesis (in German) on the relation of David Hume's philosophy to his history. The thesis won the special prize awarded to the best German prose stylist among the graduating students of the year.

My father's native language was Yiddish, but at school in Koenigsberg he appears to have rapidly learned to look down on that language as a kind of bastard German, and he never again spoke it willingly nor did he encourage his children to learn it or to show any interest in it. For him the language of Jewish culture was Hebrew, not Yiddish, and I was brought up with an anti-Yiddish bias, not as the result of any conscious depreciation of Yiddish on my father's part but as the result of the silence and implied scorn with which he treated it. The Polish and Yiddish part of his life he put resolutely behind him, and I know virtually nothing of it. But he did talk of his student days in Germany at the beginning of the century, and I have a clear picture of him then as a studious and dedicated young man, avoiding the nonsense of German student ritual, but enjoying his glass of beer and his cigar, moving quietly and determinedly, in the lively and colourful Berlin of the 1900s. He was a fine figure of a man, not tall, but well built, with abundant black hair swept back from his high forehead, a carefully shaped brown moustache and a neat Van Dyke beard. I sometimes wonder whether during his student days he ever had any doubts about his ability to reconcile orthodox Judaism with modern secular culture, whether his philosophical studies ever momentarily shook his faith in the truth or efficacy of the rabbinical view of life. There is just the faintest suggestion of the dandy in the few early photographs of my father, which sorts oddly with his idealism and sense of dedication. Perhaps he had a struggle; perhaps there was no simple continuity between his Jewish childhood and his adult ambitions as a rabbi, but a period of doubt and hesitation lay between. This is mere speculation; what is definite is that he emerged from his student days in Germany a passionately serious and dedicated young man.

I have before me as I write a notebook of my father's dated May 15, 1908. It is marked: 'Kant and Judaism. Notes', and it contains notes he made on this subject while reading in the British Museum, after he had settled in England and the year before he married. The notes are mostly in English, but occasionally he breaks into German. My father admired Kant, but was annoyed with him for his sharp criticisms of Judaism: in these notes he quotes from Kant's criticisms of Judaism and sketches out heads of a reply. Here is a characteristic extract:

> Religion des guten Lebenswandel. Christianity true Religion. But Judaism is the Religion des guten Lebenswandel. Nearly all the religious commands concern life. Even to *love* God (which Kant makes such a fuss of). It never commands one to *believe*, as Christianity does. Believing (in his Godhead) saves according to the teaching of Christ. According to Jewish Law only doing right, moral (religious) actions save man. Why does not Kant see and acknowledge it. He idealises Christianity and does Judaism great injustice by misrepresenting (perhaps misunderstanding) its tenets.

Or again:

> 'Thou shalt and thou shalt not. I am the Lord.' He admits that there is a combat between the good and the evil principle. How can we expect a final victory of the good principle if not by interference of the transcendental moral power. The Divine Maker of man who takes care to enlighten man and to indicate to him the right path (of true morality) which he is bound

to go. God the objective maker and adviser of man, also his judge and the framer of his destiny. He has revealed His will, His law to man, just in order that it should act as the 'vehicle' which Kant takes the Christian Church to be. Christ never said anything against this.

The notebook ends with a list of German references (books and articles), followed by: 'W. Wallace, "Kant", p. 74: "The old man, so courageous in his books, was a coward before his King. Let age and infirmity plead for him; and let his teaching wipe away the evil of his example."'

In his essay 'Kant and Judaism', which appeared in his book, *Aspects of Judaism*, published in 1928, my father wrote:

> That Kant himself had no adequate knowledge of, or even a proper understanding for, the teachings and traditions of Judaism has been pointed out by Dr Julius Guttman in a monograph on 'Kant und das Judentum' (Leipzig, 1908) and by the present writer in a critical contribution to the first issue of the new *Jewish World* (April 16, 1913). But Kant's inability to understand and appreciate the tenets of Judaism has never prevented Jews from understanding and appreciating the philosophy of Kant, and today it is admitted by those who combine in themselves a thorough knowledge of Jewish teaching with a full appreciation of Kant's philosophical theories that there is no religious system which is so compatible with that philosopher's epistemology as well as with his ethical doctrines as the system embodied in Judaism.

And so my father's lovers' quarrel with Kant, like his earlier one with Hume, was eventually resolved, and the resolution is in some sense a symbol of his life.

What was my father's relation to *his* father? My grandfather migrated to England while my father was still a student, to become rabbi of an orthodox Jewish congregation — the Beth Hamedrash Hagadol — in Leeds, and from that time on my father regarded Britain as his true home. He already knew English perfectly, and after a few years in

England spoke it perfectly, while my grandfather never mastered more than the merest rudiments of the language. He and my grandmother represented for me a picturesque old world in which I was not really at home. My father mediated between their world and my own, translating my grandfather's Yiddish (my grandmother could speak English) and trying to interpret the behaviour of an Edinburgh schoolboy to the old man; yet I had the feeling that my father, for all his tremendous sense of family pride and loyalty and for all the great mutual affection between him and my grandfather, was not altogether happy in seeing us in this old world atmosphere. He looked forward, to a Judaism no less orthodox but less involved with memories of the Ghetto. We went rarely to see our grandfather. I may be quite wrong, but I have a suspicion that my father preferred to keep us apart.

The house in Leeds where my grandfather lived was one of a row of small nineteenth-century brick dwellings, all exactly alike, in which a number of *nouveau* middle class hangers-on of the Industrial Revolution had once proclaimed their precarious gentility. The street had a run-down look when I knew it, and it was inhabited by very small business men or by miscellaneous oddities of firm respectability but moderate means. It was the kind of street one can see today in any British industrial town, shabby and tired looking, but determinedly decent. Behind the front door of any one of its houses one expected to hear thick Yorkshire accents proclaiming phrases out of J.B. Priestley or Eric Knight.

But number 6 was different. The brass plate read, in letters almost too worn to be legible, 'Rabbi J.H. Daiches' — the 'J' should have been 'I' as it stood for 'Israel', but my grandfather considered the letters 'I' and 'J' interchangeable — and if you pushed open the gate and went up the narrow path that skirted the tiny apology for a front garden to the front door you were aware of approaching the entrance to a very different world from that of industrial Yorkshire. It was, one might say, an emanation which seemed to be coming out of the house, a smell perhaps, a feeling, an atmosphere. And if you entered and went through the dark bead curtain into the small entrance hall and smelled the mingled odour of cigar smoke and Jewish cooking you had left Yorkshire very far behind.

My grandfather as I knew him was a benevolently patriarchal figure with twinkling eyes and a white beard. Only recently an old man who had known him in his prime told me that in his younger days in Poland he had been known for his neat clothes and well-groomed appearance, and that he had given scandal to the orthodox by sending his children (my father and my uncle) to secular non-Jewish schools and universities. Between afternoon and evening services (*minchah* and *ma'arev*) at the synagogue he would go for a walk with a certain Christian civic official, with whom he would converse in Russian — a habit which caused much shaking of heads among the older people. This new light on my grandfather came as an astonishing revelation to me, who had always considered him as belonging to a Ghetto world of Jewish piety and Jewish isolation. But evidently he too was a pioneer in his day, and tried to reconcile tradition with progress.

I saw no sign of that as a child, however. I had to watch my every movement in my grandfather's house, in case I unwittingly offended against his sense of what was proper Jewish behaviour. I could never leave my head uncovered for a moment, for example. At home we always covered our heads to pray, and to say grace before and after meals, but we were never expected to keep our heads covered continually. My father wore a black skull cap when receiving members of his congregation in his study, but as the years went by he developed the habit of keeping it in his pocket throughout much of the day and diving hastily for it when the bell rang. In his father's presence he wore it continually. I remember once, seeing the two of them together in my grandfather's house, thinking how young and *modern* my father looked beside the white bearded older rabbi. Yet at home in Edinburgh I had so often thought my father old-fashioned in manner and dress, with his black frock-coat, stiff shirt front and bow tie, and his rather formal eighteenth-century English.

In the house at Leeds the slightest daily activity seemed to partake of ritual. The great stone kitchen in the basement, where my grandmother presided amid rows of shining copper vessels, was like something out of Grimm's fairy tales, and even the dining-room, with its long narrow table running up the length of the room and its black horsehair sofa on one side (how the horsehair used to scratch my bare legs!) seemed more than a dining-room to me. My grandfather used to shuffle in in his carpet slippers before dinner and take his place at the head of the table, where there was laid out for him a special little cloth on which were a bottle of cognac, a plate of sliced pickled herring, and a loaf of dark rye bread. He would fill himself a tot of brandy and drink it off at a gulp; then he would cut a slice of bread and eat it with the herring; and then his special cloth with everything on it was removed and the meal proper (which my grandfather hardly touched) could start. I would watch this ritual with pure admiration from my place on the horsehair sofa (which was placed along one side of the table, so that we children could sit there, side by side, when having our meals: I suppose we must have been propped on something, but I don't remember that). Together with the admiration went a sense of the mystical strangeness of it all. Once, when I was almost grown up, I ventured to remark that I, too, liked pickled herring. My grandfather expressed the utmost astonishment and passed me the plate, and would not take anything himself until I had eaten rather more than I really wanted.

When I was a child I knew no Yiddish except the occasional word, referring to some aspect of daily Jewish practice, which had found its way into our ordinary discourse, and an occasional phrase such as 'Ich vaiss nisht' ('I don't know'). It was only after I had learned German, in my last years at school, that I acquired any degree of facility with the language, and even then such Yiddish as I spoke was more German than Yiddish. (It is significant that my father took an interest in and encouraged my learning of German, but took no steps whatever to help me learn Yiddish.) When I conversed with my grandfather, which was not often, we used simple Hebrew until I was in my teens, when he spoke in his native Yiddish and I replied in my Germanised form of the language. Lionel and I also used to write occasional letters to our grandfather in Hebrew. Most of them were expressions of thanks for a birthday present (generally a pound note) and I still remember the typical opening of such letters (I am transliterating roughly the Ashkenazi pronunciation): '*Hin'ni nowsein es towdosi be'ad ha'matonoh shaisholachto li*' — 'Behold I send my thanks for the gift which you have sent me.' Later on, when I had read some of the Hebrew letters of Achad Ha'am, I would vary this opening with elegant locutions learned from him, such as: '*Kabail no es towdosi . . .*' — 'Receive I pray thee my thanks . . .' and I learned too, also from Achad Ha'am, a fine opening with which to begin a letter that should have been written some time ago. It began 'Forgive, I pray thee, that on account of my abundant business I have delayed writing until now . . .' The phrase, beginning as it did with the familiar penitential phrase *s'lach no*, reminded me of the service of the Day of Atonement: and it did not seem altogether improper to address my grandfather in those terms. Yet his conversations with me violently contradicted the impression of an aloof patriarchal character with which I could not help associating him in general. He had a great fondness for low jokes. I knew that he was the world's leading authority on the Jerusalem Talmud (to be distinguished from the more popular Babylonian Talmud), and that he had produced a noble edition of it with a large Hebrew commentary surrounding a tiny island of original text; so I naturally expected words of profound wisdom to fall from his venerable lips. Instead, he would inquire whether I went to the bathroom in order to drink brandy and smoke cigars secretly, or he would suggest that the sixty-five-year-old charwoman was pining for me to take her to the pictures.

I would come into his study to find him stroking his beard and poring over a huge Hebrew tome, looking the very quintessence of rabbinic grandeur. I was prepared for him to throw a question at me concerning my Hebrew knowledge and had even got up one side of a long dialogue in that language on which I was ready to embark if only he would give me the opportunity. But when I appeared he would close his book, ask me to bring him a cigar from the cupboard (like my father, he would smoke nothing but the choicest Havanas, which he got as presents from members of his congregation), and proceed to make joking or teasing remarks about kilts and bagpipes, or about girls, or clothes, or other unrabbinical subjects. Yet as soon as I left the room he was at his book again, and I could see him through the window from the back garden, with his hand on his beard and his head nodding gently, reading and meditating.

He lived in what seemed to me an almost feudal fashion. His salary must have been quite small, and in any case when I knew him he had, I believe, virtually retired, but he had retainers who would come and see him and bring cigars or a bottle of brandy or an occasional duck or chicken. He had absolutely no money sense. My grandmother ran the financial affairs of the household, and when she died a not very efficient elderly couple came to live with him and look after things. Every time I visited him he would want to present me with a large cheque, and had to be restrained by my father or some other watchful grown-up. He was quite capable of giving me a cheque for much more than he had in the bank for I don't think he ever knew how much he had in the bank — or indeed exactly what a bank was supposed to do. My impression is that, at least in his later years, much of his income was paid in kind, and he had little occasion to handle money.

He visited us in Edinburgh only once, on the occasion of my brother Lionel's *barmitzvah* in March 1924. My father placed his study at my grandfather's disposal, and he would sit there most of the day with one of my father's Hebrew books. I was eleven and a half at the time, and in the midst of a wave of enthusiasm for things Hebrew and rabbinic. I was disconcerted to find that when my father sent me in to recite my Hebrew verbs to my grandfather, he interrupted me before I was fairly started and the whole thing was turned into a joke. I think now that he did not want me to feel an obligation to be serious and show off my Hebrew knowledge when I was with him; he wanted to try and get to know his grandchildren and not to be simply a criterion of piety and scholarship for them. But we never really got to know each other; my father's optimistic faith in the importance and the viability of British Jewish orthodoxy, his resolute repudiation of Yiddish and its Ghetto associations, stood between my grandfather and his grandchildren.

In my grandfather's last years he led a retired and lonely life, never leaving his house — indeed, scarcely stirring from the big table in his study where he sat and read and dozed all day. He became too feeble to walk to the synagogue, and on Friday nights and Saturdays a dozen or so cronies would come and conduct services in his study. It was my grandmother's death that finally confirmed him in his retirement; though he lived some twelve years longer I don't think he left the house once after her funeral. When I was a student at Oxford I used to visit him on my way back to Edinburgh, and I had the feeling that the modern world, towards which he had once made such important gestures of friendship, had finally become too much for him and he had given up the attempt to keep up with it. Yet he, to me for so long the representative of the very essence of rigid old-fashioned Jewish piety, had started out as something of a rebel; by his decision on how to educate his children he had shaped the pattern both of my father's life and of my own.

The modern world caught up with both of them, my grandfather and my father. If my grandfather retreated from it in his old age, my father, with his optimistic belief in the progressive waning of anti-Semitism and the emergence of Judaism as a proud and respected part of a pluralistic European culture, was equally baffled when the rise of Hitler put the clock back in Europe. He watched with horror and incredulity the disappearance of the Germany he knew and admired — the Germany of Goethe and Kant and Beethoven — and could never understand what had really happened. True, the events of the 1930s would have confirmed him in his devotion to Britain if any such confirmation had been required, and it did intensify his feeling for Scotland, one of the few countries in Europe, he would often declare, where the Jews had never been persecuted (though he knew that the reason for this was at least partly that the Jews reached Scotland relatively late in European history and in small numbers). But there were rumblings of fascist agitation even in Scotland; they didn't, it is true, amount to much and they represented a negligible minority of the people, but they disturbed and angered my father. He would keep an eagle eye open for letters or articles in the Scottish press which showed any trace of sympathy with the Hitlerite position, and he would reply to each with a forceful and eloquent letter to the editor. This was but an extension of his normal vigilance on behalf of the good name of the Jews in Scotland. His letters to *The Scotsman*, putting the Jewish position whenever it required to be put and always assuming the closest natural sympathy between Scottish Presbyterians and Jews, had been a feature of that newspaper since 1919. He had developed the art of Jewish apologetics to a fine point; his letters combined the shrewdness of a lawyer trained on talmudic argument with the ringing eloquence of a preacher and the moral passion of a prophet. His letters to *The Scotsman* on such subjects as Zionism, the activities of Christian missions among Jews, the position of the Jews in Europe and in Scotland in particular, Jewish ritual slaughter, anti-Semitism, and on any topical subject with reference to which the Jewish position required defence or explanation, became perhaps my father's best known claim to fame: they were read and admired throughout Scotland, and they did an immense amount to create a pro-Jewish public opinion in the country. The other day a railway official at Waverley Station, in

Edinburgh, was checking my sleeper reservation on a train out of the city and his eye was caught by the name. 'Any relation of the late rabbi?' he asked. 'I always used to read his letters in *The Scotsman*.'

My father enjoyed his role as a public figure and played it superbly. In his letters to the press his voice rang with the authority and the dignity of an official spokesman of his people, and similarly at public meetings in Edinburgh and throughout Scotland — at Masonic Lodges, the Dunfermline Business Men's Club, the League of Nations Union, Burns Clubs — he would present with eloquence and passion the Jewish view of the subject under discussion. He had not been long in Edinburgh before he became known as one of the city's most distinguished public speakers, who could be counted on to make forceful oratorical contributions to any humanitarian or liberal cause. Of course he spoke too at Zionist meetings and at Jewish fund-raising occasions of all kinds, and looking back I seem to see an endless round of such occasions, but I think it was the speeches he made as a representative Jewish spokesman before non-Jewish and mixed audiences that gave him most satisfaction. For that, in his view, was an important part of the function of the modern Orthodox Jewish rabbi — to speak up for his people with dignity and equality before his fellow citizens.

This side of my father's activities can perhaps best be summed up by quoting four letters to him that I have found among a mass of his miscellaneous papers. Here is the first:

LODGE QUEEN'S EDINBURGH RIFLES
(THE ROYAL SCOTS)
NO. 1253
'Mansfield', 74 Fergus Drive, Glasgow, NW
20th December, 1935

Rev. Dr Salis Daiches
17 Crawfurd Road
Edinburgh, 9

Reverend Sir and Brother,

I was very pleased to learn from our Secretary that you had accepted our invitation to give the oration at our Burns Festival. I must thank you very much for the honour you are doing us and I am looking forward to meeting you again on that evening.

> With cordial greetings,
> Yours sincerely and fraternally,
> Alex Mennie

The second is from the editor of the *Edinburgh Evening News*. My father had evidently written to him offering congratulations on some anniversary either of the paper or of the editor personally:

EDINBURGH EVENING NEWS
18 Market Street, Edinburgh 1
12 *February*, 1936

Rev. Dr Salis Daiches, A.M, Ph.D.
17 Crawfurd Road
Edinburgh, 9

Dear Rabbi

You have sent me a wonderful letter of congratulation, full of encouragement and good will. I appreciate especially what you say about the Jewish community in Scotland and in my own town of Edinburgh. I know I have many friends among the Jews, and if at any time there is anything I can do to help their cause, you have only to come up here.

I am sure Mrs McPhail will be very pleased with the very kind letter you have sent us.

> With every kind wish,
> I remain yours sincerely
> Walter McPhail, Editor

The third is more routine, and typical of hundreds:

THE LEAGUE OF NATIONS UNION
(Greenock Branch)
Hon. Secretary Mr J.W. Ashford 18 Kilbain Street,
Greenock.

Phone no. 118

Rev. dear Sir,

Thank you for your letter. My Committee has not yet
fixed a date for the Annual Meeting, but would be pleased
to arrange a date suitable to you . . .

The first time I am in Edinburgh, I shall make a point
of seeing you.

With thanks, I am, Yours truly,
J.W. Ashford, Hon. Secretary

Across the foot of this letter my father has written the date,
'17th March,' and on that day he addressed the Greenock
Branch of the League of Nations Union.

The fourth letter is in many ways the most interesting:

NIDDRIE MAINS WORKERS' INSTITUTE
17 Harewood Drive, Craigmillar, Edinburgh.
2nd December, 1935

Dear Sir,

I have been instructed to write and ask you, if you would
kindly permit an interview to the above organisation. We
are a body of workers in the area, who have up to the
present time been raising to build a hall.

Sir we intend to commence the building in about a
months time, the interview is for the porpose (*sic*) of asking
you to honour our attempt at the opening cermoney (*sic*)
and cutting of first turf for us.

Hoping to be able to explain our aims and object to you
in our interview.

I am yours sincerely
J.P. Ferguson, Secy.

My father did in due course cut the first turf for the new workers' hall, and I think few things gave him more satisfaction.

If this side of my father's activities took him considerably beyond the path of duty trod by my grandfather in the performance of the more traditional activities of a Jewish rabbi, it must not be thought for a moment that my father in any way neglected those traditional activities. He would receive almost daily visits from the older members of his congregation in search of guidance on some intricate matter of Jewish law: whether a chicken could be considered kosher if a pin had been found stuck in some delicate part of its internal organs or what was the correct procedure on the part of a bachelor who wanted to get out of marrying his deceased brother's widow. These matters he dealt with scrupulously and conscientiously, becoming on such occasions the old-fashioned administrator of rabbinical law in all its logical nicety. His very appearance seemed to change when he gave an audience of this kind: he allowed his shoulders to hunch forward a little and spoke, reluctantly and in his Germanised fashion, the Yiddish which was the speech of his visitor; and of course his skull cap was always on his head. This side of him was always uppermost when he spoke to the older, foreign-born members of his congregation: with the native-born generation he was brisker and altogether more modern; the sing-song tones of talmudic exposition gave way to a more resounding rhetorical note or to the reasonable 'let's-argue-this-out-together' tone of twentieth-century inquiry.

Before my father came to Edinburgh there were two Jewish congregations in the city, one consisting entirely of older, foreign-born members whose native language was Yiddish, and the other, though also orthodox, having a considerable proportion of Scottish-born members who did not believe that to practise Judaism meant to duplicate exactly the kind of life their fathers had led in the East European ghetto. My father made it a condition of accepting his 'call' that it should come jointly from both congregations, and when he arrived in Edinburgh his first task was to weld the two into a unity. For some years they continued to worship in different synagogues, that of the foreign-born group being an old and draughty hall in what was pretty much a slum area of the city. The other synagogue, a converted chapel in Graham Street, clearly represented the wave of the future, and its congregation grew while the other's declined. My father would worship and preach on Saturdays at the Graham Street *shul*, though he would visit the other (known as the Central *shul*) at regular intervals and preach there in Yiddish. After a few years the Central *shul* closed down and Graham Street accommodated both congregations. My father's real ambition was to build a splendid new synagogue in a pleasant part of the city, a synagogue which could easily accommodate all the Jews in Edinburgh and would in addition have an attached *Beth Hamedrash* where the older and more traditional members could pray three times daily and conduct their talmudic study circle. This ambition was finally realised after immense effort, and the new synagogue in Salisbury Road was opened with full civic honours in 1932. Its opening was a high point in my father's career, for here was represented the union of the old and the new in a common Jewish orthodoxy; the building took its place worthily amid the architecture of Edinburgh and signified that Edinburgh Jews played their part with integrity and dignity and with the respect of their neighbours in the life of their city. The shadows cast by Hitler's Germany were soon to obscure the Jewish horizon completely; after 1934 there was little cause for optimism even among men as naturally optimistic as my father. 1934, too, was the year when he and my mother celebrated their silver wedding, the year when we moved into a new house, the first my father had ever owned, and the year when I graduated with first class honours at Edinburgh University, to my father's immense satisfaction. So altogether the years 1932 to 1934 represent the watershed, as it were, of my father's career. After that, the world he had counted on began to disappear beneath his feet; anti-semitism, which I had been brought up to believe was a phenomenon of the bad old days that would never recur, would rise to unprecedented heights in Germany, and I myself began for the first time to doubt profoundly the whole basis of the creed in which I had been brought up. (Perhaps I should interpolate here that that basis, from a belief in which my father apparently never deviated one jot throughout his life, was that the Law was given to Moses by divine revelation on Mount Sinai, that this revelation was unique, and central in human history, and that the function of the Jewish people had been to receive and transmit and would be to foster and develop the revealed Law.)

It had been a hard climb to the summit represented by the opening of the new synagogue. The position which my father had won for himself, and through himself for his people in Scotland, was achieved by the continual expenditure of energy, writing, speaking, debating, counselling, planning, being diplomatic here and righteously indignant there, moving continuously between platform, pulpit, study, and meeting room. Our house was in some respects like a public institution; callers were liable to arrive at any time. My father had to keep up a style of living which his modest salary made extremely difficult. The Edinburgh Hebrew Congregation was small — about four hundred families, two thousand souls — and not wealthy, and could not afford to pay its spiritual leader much of a stipend. My father, in virtue of his personality and abilities, had made himself the unofficial spiritual leader of all Jews in Scotland; but in sober fact he was but the rabbi of a small congregation. The result of this was that while the outside world regarded him as the Jewish equivalent of the Archbishop of Canterbury or at least of the Moderator of the Church of Scotland, and expected him to live accordingly, my father had to manage somehow on his small income. We had to live in a large and thoroughly genteel house in a residential part of the city, we had to dress well, we had to subscribe decently to public charities. My father was thus always harassed by financial worries, always haunted by unpaid bills. And though somehow the bills always got paid eventually and no visible sign of financial stringency was ever open to the public eye, the continuous strain must have worn down both my parents.

There was another kind of strain, more wearing than financial worry. My father, in the course of his successful attempt to make himself a real leader of his people and to build up a public conception of the Jew in Scotland as the respected member of an important element in a pluralistic culture, aroused some bitter jealousies and made some implacable enemies. A number of petty busybodies who had made a profession of exploiting disputes among different sections of the community were taken aback at my father's policy of uniting all the Jews of Edinburgh into one congregation (it was, indeed, a unique policy and the Edinburgh Hebrew Congregation remains a unique Jewish congregation in Britain) and deliberately set out to make trouble for him. I remember one or two strange and dramatic episodes, but they were less serious than the continual attempts to undermine my father's position, to discredit him in the eyes of Jew and Christian alike, that this small group kept making for some years. My father, who had conducted his side of the business with a fine dignity, won in the end, as he was bound to, though for some years a small group of malcontents worshipped separately in a hired room (known among the other Edinburgh Jews as 'the Bolshie *shul*') in a mood of spiteful piety.

All this, of course, was worrying, but most worrying of all was the affair that became known as 'the Levison case'. One day in the 1920s a gentleman calling himself Rabbi Levinson turned up in Edinburgh and made contact with the members of the 'Bolshie *shul*'. He began to make large claims about his rabbinical distinction and jurisdiction, and eventually my father, after making some investigations into the man's character and history, denounced him as a trouble-making impostor and wrote a letter to the London *Jewish Chronicle* pointing out that 'Rabbi' Levison was no rabbi and warning British Jews against him. (At least, I think that is what happened, but it may be that the *Chronicle* came to the same conclusion independently: it certainly published a warning against Levison.) Levison then proceeded to bring an action for libel against both my father and the *Jewish Chronicle*. This was an immense shock to my father, who knew perfectly well that Levison was a rogue and an impostor but knew also that this would not be easy to prove in a court of law. And of course my father had no money to fight a legal action. But the action had to be fought, and my father engaged the best legal representatives available, trusting that he would win and be awarded costs. As the case proceeded Levison's counsel submitted as evidence of his being a genuine rabbi a large number of documents, some of them signed by rabbinical authorities of international reputation. All these were testimonials to the scholarship, piety, and rabbinic distinction of Levison. When my father's counsel saw these documents, he thought the case was over: what answer could there be to such evidence? My father, however, persuaded his counsel to ask leave to borrow the documents for a week (they had been deposited in court), and leave was granted. He read them over very carefully, and as he read he noticed a number of things. One of the most impressive documents was signed by Rabbi Kook, the late Chief Rabbi of Palestine. Now my father knew Rabbi Kook, and corresponded with him; in fact, he had a letter from him on his desk at that time. He compared the signature of his own letter with that on the document brought by Levison, and found that the two were quite different. A closer investigation made it clear that both the signature and the seal were forged. With this clue in his possession, my father went carefully through the other documents. Many of them were clearly genuine; but these did not prove anything except that the writer thought Levison was a nice man. But every one of the documents purporting to come from a rabbinical authority was suspect. One purported to come from a town in Poland which my father was sure did not exist. Another came from the head of a continental *Yeshivah* (rabbinical college) that he had never heard of. One was supposed to be from a rabbi in some small town in the interior of Australia.

My father informed his counsel that in his view all the Levison documents which seemed to prove that he was in fact a genuine rabbi were either forged or had been tampered with; the numerous others which were genuine doing no harm to my father's case at all. The eminent legal authority at first refused to believe this. No man, he protested, could be guilty of such criminal folly. But my father insisted, and urged that before the documents were returned to court they should be photostated for further study. This was done, under protest from the legal advisers. Soon afterwards, Levison asked for leave to take the documents temporarily out of court, as he was applying for a position with a Jewish congregation in Wales and needed the testimonials. He was given leave to withdraw them for a short period. When they were put back, as they were a week or so later, my father asked his counsel to borrow them again, briefly. What, asked the advocate, could he possibly want with them again? My father pressed the point, and the documents were soon in his hands again. He noticed at once that the bundle felt lighter. He examined them carefully: every one of the forged and suspect documents had gone! When my father rang up his lawyer to tell him this, the good man was at first incredulous, but seeing was believing, and he was soon brought to realise what had happened. What had happened, of course, was that Levison, when he heard that my father had been examining the documents, realised that he might have discovered the forgeries and thought it prudent, even at the risk of destroying his case, to withdraw them. What he did not know was that my father and his defending counsel had photographs of all the documents he had originally submitted.

Well might my father have said, in biblical and Cromwellian phrase, 'The Lord has delivered him into my hand.' For that was the beginning of the end of Levison, whose defence crumpled when faced with the fact of the missing documents. When my father's counsel drew the attention of the judge in court to the absence from the returned bundle of the very documents which he was prepared to prove were forgeries, the judge sharply asked Levison for an explanation. Levison said that the missing testimonials and diplomas had been accidentally destroyed by his landlady when she was clearing up his room. The coincidence of the landlady's having accidentally destroyed just those documents which my father was prepared to prove were forgeries was too much for anybody to credit, and it was not long before Levison was completely exposed and the case was concluded. Judgment, with costs, was awarded to my father, and the judge said some severe words about the behaviour of Levison's solicitor.

This was, of course, a very satisfactory conclusion for my father. Before the discovery that the forged documents were missing, the court was preparing to send out a commission of inquiry to interrogate the persons alleged to have given these testimonials to Levison — and this could have cost my father a fortune, though presumably it would have been charged to Levison if my father had won and been awarded costs. But though my father did win and was awarded costs, Levison skipped the country (it was thought that he went to America) and avoided paying a penny, so that eventually my father's solicitors had to come back to him to settle the bill. Fortunately, the *Jewish Chronicle*, who had been joint defendants with my father and who had been cleared as a result of my father's astuteness in handling the matter, recognised what they owed to him and offered to settle his legal expenses — an offer which was gratefully accepted.

Throughout the long months during which the Levison case dragged on, my father continued to fulfil all his normal duties, preaching, lecturing, writing, advising. We children had no idea at the time of the great weight of anxiety that must have been pressing upon him. We knew all about the case, but we thought of it as something thrilling and amusing. It never occurred to us that if by any chance my father had lost, his whole reputation and career would have been ruined, his whole life's ambitions destroyed. I remember seeing the photographed documents lying on his desk in his study and reading through some of them with casual interest: I recollect some brief notes to the effect that Levison had successfully performed circumcisions. And I remember one evening my father sitting in his chair by the fire after dinner, stroking his moustache in the way he had and looking unusually worried. But for the most part he gave no sign of the strain upon him. Even at the end, with the enormous relief of the judgment, he remained calm and went on with his arduous daily duties. His victory was another proof of the rightness of his way of life, proof that God would not see the righteous forsaken. As for me, I never doubted that my father would win — I took it as a matter of course — and when I heard of the judgement there came into my head the sentence I had read in history books, spoken by loyal subjects after the execution of a traitor: 'So perish all the King's enemies!'

Long after the Levison case was over it continued to provide my father with an enthralling after-dinner story, with which he would regale guests. He would tell it well, building up carefully to the climax of the discovery of the forged documents and letting the tension die away somewhat before he came to the second climax, the discovery of the absence of the suspected documents from the returned bundle. My father took a naïve pride in his own part in it all, and stressed the fact that his counsel was reluctant to borrow the documents in the first place and still more so to borrow them a second time. I last heard him tell the story in December 1944, when I was home briefly on leave from a war job. It was a Friday night, and there were guests at dinner, including the Senior Jewish Chaplain to the Forces, Rabbi Brodie (now Chief Rabbi of the British Empire). I had heard my father tell the story many times before, but it never became tedious to me. This time I heard it with peculiar pleasure: I was on my first visit back to Edinburgh in five years, having been cut off on the other side of the Atlantic by the war and being able to get back now only because I was flown across the Atlantic on British Government service by the R.A.F. Transport Command. It was like old days again — Friday night, guests for dinner, my father telling of the Levison case. I noticed, however, that he got one or two of the details wrong, and though he corrected himself, he had not the firm grip on the story that he used to have. I looked across the table at him: his right arm was in plaster, the result of a nasty fracture he had received some weeks before when he had been knocked down by a lorry while about to board a tram-car; his face showed heavy lines of fatigue, and his voice too sounded tired. I did not know then that he was a dying man, and would live only a few more months. But I did reflect how satisfactory it was that the greatest threat to his career had long passed into the realm of anecdote, and I thought that Hitler, too, was now in sight of his end and looked forward to the time when this black shadow would pass completely from the Jewish sky and my father could relax at last in a world that showed, in spite of everything, the eventual triumph of right over might. That phrase, 'the triumph of right over might', was a favourite one of my father's and he used it often during the war. He died on 2 May, 1945, one day after Hitler and three weeks after Roosevelt.

CHAPTER SIX

There were only three years between my elder brother Lionel and my younger sister Sylvia: I came in the middle, exactly as much younger than Lionel as I was older than Sylvia. My middle position had certain advantages. Lionel was the one who had to pioneer the new situations, and I followed where he had been. He was a year ahead of me at school, and encountered new subjects and new masters a year before I did, so that by the time I had to face them they were familiar to me from innumerable descriptions and anecdotes. Sometimes I even had Lionel's notes in front of me when a teacher was giving a new lesson; I remember on one occasion having on the desk before me a set of the superb history summaries that Dr Brydon, one of the finest teachers of History to schoolboys who ever lived, used to put on the blackboard. I had got the summaries from Lionel, who had been in Dr Brydon's class the year before, and was able to answer every question in exactly the form which the master wanted. He soon discovered that I had an old set of his notes, and cheerfully allowed me to display my knowledge by starting a sentence and then turning to me to finish it (*e.g.*, Brydon: 'The first defect in the Congress of Vienna was —' He turned to me. Me: 'It ignored the rising claims of national feeling.') This sort of thing was of course useful, though it grew progressively less so as I went up the school and grew more independent in my attitude to the various subjects. Other advantages of being the middle child were that I was in some degree insulated from the emotional pressure that parents in spite of themselves direct against the oldest and the youngest among their children, and that

I was on the whole left more to myself. I was the youngest (or rather, the younger) for not quite eighteen months, and then Sylvia was born, the first girl, and a remarkably pretty one at that, with the result that any claims I had to special attention disappeared at once. Not that I was ever conscious of being less attended to than Lionel or Sylvia; but I think, on looking back, that in some subtle ways I probably was.

There is, in Jewish tradition as in many other traditions, a peculiar *mystique* attached to the oldest son. Lionel was the first-born male, and as such he had certain privileges that I was denied. I can hear now my father's voice saying: 'Lionel should do it: he is the eldest.' Duties as well as privileges were involved, and I don't think Lionel cared particularly for either. I grew used to the notion that Lionel was in the nature of things more privileged than I, and, unless my memory deceives me, I very rarely resented this. Perhaps I did, though, unconsciously; else why should I have so often prided myself secretly on my greater sensitivity to my father's moods and ideals? There was a significant difference in temperament between Lionel and myself. At school he was indolent and unambitious, while I worked hard and was always anxious to excel. He got out of as many religious duties as he could, although, of course, during the period of our childhood he no more than the rest of us would have thought of actively defying orthodox standards by riding on a tramcar on a Saturday or eating improper food. Praying, for example: we were expected to *daven* (pray) regularly and at length each morning, and, after we had reached the age of thirteen, lay *tephillin* (put on phylacteries) and go through the whole vast series of morning prayers before breakfast. Lionel, who always got up at the last possible moment, gabbled through the *Sh'ma* (the most important of these prayers, but very short) in record time, and let it go at that. I felt an absolute obligation to start at the very beginning and go right through to the end without missing a word. It was a psychological compulsion, of the kind that made Dr Johnson touch every second lamppost as he walked through the streets of London, and had little to do with piety. If by negligence or haste I found I had omitted even a word, I felt I had to go back to the beginning and start the whole thing over again. I reached the stage where I could rush through some sixty pages of Hebrew in ten minutes flat, without distorting a single word (the pages, I admit, were the small duodecimo pages of Singer's prayer book).

I also felt a certain compulsion to be at the Saturday morning service at the very beginning, though few people came or were expected to come at the start, and the larger part of the congregation arrived for the 'Reading of the Law', which was a good halfway through the proceedings. It was, like all Jewish services except the pleasant Friday night one (always my favourite for its plaintive melodies as well as its sensible length), long, beginning about 9.30 and going on until about 12.00. My father, of course, had to be there at the beginning, and I always liked to go with him. Lionel, who got up later, used to arrive about 10 o'clock. My father never liked this separate arrival of Lionel and me, and was not particularly eager for me to come so early. Once, I remember, as I was preparing to start out with him, he suggested that I stay and wait for Lionel, so that we would both arrive together. I think I was eleven or so at the time. The suggestion upset me, for some reason I felt unable to explain, and when my father repeated that he expected me to wait and come later with Lionel, I found myself, inexplicably, bursting into tears. I am not quite sure what my emotions really were — nothing so simple as frustrated piety. I had set my heart on going with my father and being in *shul* for the beginning of the service. He was astonished to find me in tears. 'What, *crying*?' he said. 'Foolish boy. Come along, then.' And I dried my tears and went along with him. After that there was never any question about it: I always went with him at the beginning.

Piety did play some part in my childhood praying, however. I made up a long prayer for myself, partly in Hebrew and partly in English, to be recited under the bedclothes after I had got into bed at night. It was a curious mixture of

echoes from the regular Hebrew night prayer with snatches
from a variety of other sources. It began with a request to be
spared bad dreams (I was cursed with horrid nightmares as a
child, and often brought my parents upstairs in a hurry with
my fearful screams), went on to recite the *Sh'ma*, continued
with bits of psalms and hymns, and ended with an original
composition in English requesting a blessing on the whole
family. It was quite a long performance altogether, and the
more tired I was the more compulsion I felt to go through
the whole thing. Sometimes, when I was exceptionally tired,
I allowed myself an abbreviated form, but in most cases I then
found my conscience (or something within me) unsatisfied
and had to proceed to the complete set of prayers after all.
Between the ages of about eleven and fifteen I became a
conscientious prayer in *shul*, making it a point of honour
not to skip anything. The real endurance test came on the
Day of Atonement, when there was an enormous collection
of prayers to be got through which hardly anybody thought
of reciting entirely: I would go through them all. It was only
in my late teens when I had examined some of the prayers
and found them superstitious or in some way offensive to
my increasingly critical mind, that I gave up the habit of
tackling the complete prayer book.

Lionel's attitude to these matters seemed to me at the
time much more careless. He did what he had to in the
way of praying and religious duties, and omitted whatever
he could get away with omitting. Not that he was at that
age in any way a sceptic; he accepted his religion easily
and naturally, but, being a schoolboy, he took the normal
schoolboy's line of doing the minimum in anything that
involved work or application.

Lionel, Sylvia, and I naturally played together a great
deal, and Lionel and I alone to an even greater extent.
His attitude to me was a mixture of loyalty and a most
exasperating teasing. He teased me sometimes to distraction.
I remember one occasion, when I was twelve or thirteen,
he amused himself by drawing up a contract in which I
was made to hand over to him something of mine that

he wanted. Naturally, I refused to sign it, so he secretly cut my signature out of the cover of my French notebook and gummed it on to the contract. This was, of course, a joke; he never intended to hold me to the contract; but when I found my French notebook mutilated — it was a new one, and I had prided myself on keeping it with scrupulous neatness — I was seized with a raging sense of injustice that vented itself in howling abuse. To my further infuriation, my parents reproved me for yelling and screaming, and seemed uninterested in the monstrous injustice I had suffered; to them, I was simply being very naughty and that was that. I remember the evening clearly: my father had been away, lecturing I think, somewhere in England, and had just returned, presenting both Lionel and me with a penknife. It was with his new penknife that Lionel cut out my name from the notebook. The atmosphere of happy family reunion was abruptly shattered by my raging on discovering the state of my notebook, and I recall thinking bitterly as, denied all redress, I went fuming upstairs to my room, that the incident had spoiled what would have been a happy evening.

On another occasion I remember that Lionel and a boy who lived in the next street (his name sticks in my mind as Bill Revans, but I may have got it wrong) jointly persuaded me to shake some pennies out of my little green money box and to spend the money on a large ice cream. Such behaviour was unthinkable in our family: we children saved our weekly pennies (later, threepenny pieces) and the idea of spending them on sweets or ice cream was shocking. I allowed myself to be persuaded, bought the ice cream, and gave Lionel and Bill Revans the bulk of it. Later that day Lionel calmly informed my father of what I had done. I think it was sheer psychological curiosity on his part; he wanted to know how my father would react; but of course I was furious at this treachery. However, my father's reaction was surprisingly mild; he simply said that I shouldn't have done it and turned to his work, and that was the end of that.

But with all his teasing Lionel was fundamentally loyal.

His sense of family unity was very deep — to this day I think he depends on it emotionally to a greater extent than any of us — and in a crisis he could always be depended on. I recall two incidents, widely separated in time, which illustrate his combination of day-to-day teasing with fundamental loyalty. The first occurred when I was about fourteen of fifteen, and was writing a great deal of verse, which I kept in a fat dark-blue notebook. Once, after I had entered a new composition in the book and was about to put it away in the drawer where I kept it, Lionel noticed what I was doing and made some offensive remark about my 'poems'. I was angered, but instead of saying anything I calmly took up the notebook again and wrote down on the last page exactly what he had said. I headed the page: 'Nasty remarks that people have made about my poems.' Lionel's curiosity was aroused, and he demanded to know what I was doing. I told him, and explained that he would look a frightful fool when I was a famous poet and the disparaging remarks that he had made about my work were revealed. To my surprise, he took my words more seriously than I myself did, and reproved me for showing a mean spirit and bearing malice: it was unfair, he protested, that casual words spoken in haste should be recorded for posterity. I was touched, and tore out the page.

The other incident occurred either in my last year at school or in my first year in Edinburgh University. I had written a number of sketches, both words and music, songs from which Lionel and I often sang to entertain guests. Lionel had the idea that one of them should actually be presented publicly on a proper stage. I protested that this was not feasible, but Lionel persisted. He went round to all the boys of our own age that we knew — which meant, in fact, a handful of sons of members of the Edinburgh Jewish community — and aroused their interest by himself singing through the whole of one of the sketches, taking all the parts in turn. I was too shy to go into any of the boys' houses, but remained outside in the street while Lionel went through his performance. He convinced enough people of the merit of the piece to have it put on by a Jewish young people's club of which we were members (the Edinburgh Junior Jewish Club it was called, and later the name was changed to the Edinburgh Young Jewish Society). Lionel collected the cast, arranged for the hire of the hall, and produced the show, with an energy and fervour unusual for him. It was a great success, and was followed the next year by another. Never once did he show the slightest jealousy of my status as author and composer: for him, the whole thing showed what the family could do.

Lionel, as I have said, was never as good at his studies as I was, either at school or at home with his Hebrew. He gave up the piano quite early because, although he was musical and had a good voice, he could not be bothered with it and had not enough natural facility with the instrument to enable him to cover up his lack of practising. But he was much better with his hands than I was, and did extra woodwork at school, a subject for which he won several prizes. He also won, year after year, the school's annual elocution prize. He had — and has — a fine voice and a clear, resonant utterance. It was not until he went to the university that he realised his natural gifts as a public speaker. Temperamentally different from my father as he was in so many ways, he inherited his rhetorical flair. In fact, we both did, though in quite different ways. Neither of us ever found any difficulty in speaking impromptu with considerable force and eloquence; if Lionel can today walk into court after half-an-hour's rapid looking over of a vast mass of papers and deliver, without a single note, a powerful and at the same time meticulously logical defence of his client, and if I can walk into a lecture room and talk for an hour, similarly without a note, on a literary subject, we both owe our talent to our father's inheritance.

In spite of the fact that Lionel was not as good at his formal studies as I was, my father always seemed to pay more attention to his progress at school and at the university. When Lionel started Greek, my father went out and bought a copy of Pope's *Homer* (a second-hand

copy from Grant's), presenting it to him with the remark
that he was never to use it as a 'crib', but only to read in
a general way after he had done his translation from the
Greek for himself. (It did not take Lionel long to discover
that it was impossible to use Pope's *Homer* as a crib!)
Lionel's career was discussed more fully and more often
than mine was. When, on one occasion, Lionel came near
enough to the top of his class at school to win a prize, my
father was so pleased that he bought him a set of chessmen,
and wrote an inscription to him in ink on the wooden box.
This outraged my sense of justice. I pointed out to my father
that I had consistently done better at school than Lionel
had, and that I had never received any recognition of that
sort; was it fair to present Lionel with a box of chessmen
for getting a prize in a 'B' class when I was regularly doing
even better in an 'A' class? My father recognised the justice
of my protest; he took out his penknife and scratched out
the 'Lionel' on the inscription, putting in its stead (with
some squeezing) 'Lionel and David'. But the wood was
rough where he had scratched it, and the ink ran. The
box still exists, with 'Lionel and David' merged into an
indeterminate blob of ink.

As I grew older, and my literary and academic interests
increased, I found more to talk about with my father than
Lionel did, and the balance was redressed. It must not be
thought that in any case there was any question of my father
deliberately paying more attention to Lionel. It was for the
most part just that he was the first-born, and he arrived at
each of the milestones of childhood progress before I did; so
naturally a greater fuss was made when he got there. There
were more and fancier cakes at his *barmitzvah* party than at
mine, and my grandfather and one of my father's sisters came
up to Edinburgh for the occasion, while nobody came up for
mine. And my father's congregation produced handsomer
presents for Lionel than they did for me. After all, when
an occasion of that sort happens a second time, the first
fine careless rapture has been lost. When, coming home
from *shul* after singing the relevant portion of the law and

prophets on my *barmitzvah* (it is traditional for a boy on attaining his *barmitzvah* to give such a performance in the synagogue), somebody congratulated me on the way I had done my part, my mother, I think quite unconsciously, said: 'Ah, but you should have heard Lionel.' Lionel probably did sing better at his *barmitzvah* than I did at mine; he had an excellent voice, and it was still a clear childish treble, while my voice, not naturally so resonant as his, was already on the point of breaking when I was thirteen; but my mother's remark, which I have never forgotten, stays in my mind as a symbol of the birthright of the first-born in a Jewish family.

All this helped to encourage my proud sense of being lonely and different, which grew upon me during my adolescence. But it did nothing to lessen that deeply affectionate and almost protective feeling toward my parents that I have already described. The image of my father as a lonely idealist in a naughty world and of my mother as a frail beauty in a dangerous world grew steadily stronger throughout my adolescent years. And for years I had a strong feeling that I, alone of us children, was destined to take the torch from my father's hand and help to transmit it down the generations. I sometimes thought of myself as Jacob and Lionel as Esau, or even of myself as Joseph, and once lay awake all night wondering whether I might not be the Messiah. Yet it is quite probable that the night after my messianic meditation, rich with all the emotions of Jewish history, I was imagining myself in full Highland dress participating (to the sound of the bagpipes) in some splendid assertion of Scotland's nationhood.

How difficult it is to tell the truth and not be misleading! It might be imagined from what I have written above that I had a grievance against Lionel for being the elder son and against my parents for treating him as such. But I had no shadow of such grievance (in spite of individual instances such as that of the chessmen) nor did I ever really believe that Lionel got preferential treatment from my parents. It was, after all, the simple fact that he *was* the eldest, and that was that. I accepted the fact with the simple pragmatism of childhood. Though I was easily stirred to a sense of injustice about little things — as most children are — the idea of a general grievance against the state of affairs would have been inconceivable to me. As a family, we were as united as a family could be, loyal, proud of each other and of our traditions, maintaining a united front against the world.

Sylvia, who often joined in our play and was very much of a tomboy as a little girl, must have had her own secret life, of which I knew nothing. She was bright at school, talkative and clear-headed at home. There was a streak of sternness in her character which developed as she grew older; she had a strong will, the kind of clear, logical mind one thinks of as masculine, and at the same time more than her share of feminine attractiveness. From an early age she learned to help Mother in the kitchen, and often when Mother was unwell she would pretty well look after the house, managing her schoolwork at the same time. Brothers, of course, never think of whether a sister is pretty or not, and I remember the shock of surprise when I saw her in her first grown-up party dress and realised how very attractive she was.

My father had old-fashioned notions about her. As he watched her develop from a lively *gamine* into a beautiful woman he thought of her marrying — at the age of about twenty-one, say — and expected that if suitable Jewish young men were brought to her attention she would fall in love with one of them. But Sylvia had an immense scorn for that whole approach to marriage. Indeed, she had an immense scorn for a lot of things. Her downright, logical mind, her ruthless intellectual honesty, her refusal to compromise an inch on any subject whatsoever, made her a most formidable debating opponent. She could see no use in the conventional hypocrisies of social life. 'Why should I talk to a man as though I liked him if I think he's a fool?' she would burst out. 'Why should I?' was one of her favourite questions. 'Why *should* I *pretend*? It's dishonest. You don't want me to be dishonest, do you?' The result was that her social manner was for a while gauche and unhappy, and she frightened to death innumerable young men. But she eventually learned to make at least some allowances for the follies of the world.

I have talked up till now as though there were only three of us children — Lionel, Sylvia, and myself. And so there were, for a long time. But when Sylvia was nearly ten and I was nearly eleven-and-a-half and Lionel almost thirteen, our sister Beryl was born, the baby of the family. She was far enough behind to seem to us of a different generation. Sylvia was maternal to her; Lionel and I were avuncular. We never thought of ourselves as four children, but as the usual three, and then Beryl. Lionel and I treated her as a sort of mascot. We raced her pram down Blackford Hill, took her scrambling over Arthur's Seat, read stories to her, fed her with fantastic information which she eagerly lapped up. When I was working for my Higher Leaving Certificate I would do my Chemistry revision aloud, and she would pick up odd facts, such as the valency of sulphur in sulphur trioxide. This encouraged me to feed her deliberately with facts and figures of this sort, which she memorised without, of course, understanding. She would astound visitors by reciting complicated chemical equations at the age of five. At the age of seven she had to write a little story about King Alfred and the cakes for school: I was then taking the British History class at the university, and I dictated to her a long disquisition about the historicity of the story and the origin of the legend, which she duly wrote down in her notebook and presented to the astonished teacher. We had immense fun with her — at least Lionel and I did. Sylvia was devoted to her in a more purely maternal way, looked after her whenever our mother was ill or busy, protected her with jealous efficiency. My father delighted in her; he would relax more in playing with her than at any other time. When she grew up she turned away from Jewish orthodoxy more rapidly than any of the rest of us had.

CHAPTER SEVEN

The morning slow train from Edinburgh to Dundee used to stop (as I suppose it still does) at many of the Fife coast towns on the way. This is why the train used to be, in the 1920s, the favourite mode of transport of those Edinburgh Jews who made a precarious living as itinerant salesmen, peddling anything from sewing needles to ready-made dresses among the good housewives and fisherfolk of Fife. They were the 'trebblers', in their own Scots–Yiddish idiom; they had come as young men from Lithuania or Poland seeking freedom and opportunity but somehow had never got on as they had planned. Those with more push and enterprise had moved westward to Glasgow and often on from there to America; a few had managed to build up flourishing businesses in Edinburgh; but the trebblers were the failures, who spent their days carrying their battered suitcases from door to door in the little grey towns of Fife, to return home in the evening with a pound or so gained to a shabby but comfortable flat in one of the more run-down districts of Edinburgh. There, in old stone buildings where the gentry and nobility of Scotland had lived in the eighteenth and early nineteenth centuries, within a stone's throw of the 'Royal Mile' with its violent and picturesque historical associations, they re-created the atmosphere of the Ghetto and lived a life of self-contained Jewish orthodoxy. Edinburgh, one of the few European capitals with no anti-semitism in its history, accepted them with characteristic cool interest. In its semi-slums they learned such English as they knew, which meant in fact that they grafted the debased Scots of the Edinburgh streets on to their native Yiddish to produce one of the most remarkable dialects ever spoken by man. (Yet not such a comically incredible speech as my American friends seem to imagine: Scots preserves many Germanic words lost in standard English and found, in a similar or even identical form, in Yiddish, as 'lift' for air (German *luft*), 'licht' for light (identical in Scots, German and Yiddish), 'hoast' for cough (German *husten*). Douglas Young has pointed out that Goethe's last words, '*mehr licht*', would have been pronounced the same in Scots, 'mair licht'; and they would be the same in Yiddish.) Their sons and daughters, making full use of the city's admirable educational facilities, grew up to be doctors and scientists and professors, changing their names from Pinkinsky to Penn, from Finkelstein to Fenton, from Turiansky to Torrence. But they themselves, the Scottish–Jewish pioneers who never quite got where they wanted to go, changed nothing. On Fridays in the winter, when the sun set early, they would be home by the middle of the afternoon, to welcome the sabbath. On Saturday, of course, as well as on all Jewish festivals, there was no 'trebbling'. And on weekdays in the Dundee train they would chant their morning prayers, strapping their phylacteries on to arm and forehead.

It was a strange thing to see, a compartment full of trebblers at their morning prayers. They were rarely interrupted by Gentiles. They had perfected a technique for getting compartments to themselves, and even if they had not, it would have taken a hardy outsider to enter a compartment where a swaying, bearded figure stood chanting at the window. Old Moishe Pinkinsky, a huge round-shouldered man with a red beard and a peculiar fierceness of gesticulation (which belied the essential gentleness of his nature), scared off many a would-be interloper. Once, however, when the train was particularly crowded, a desperate latecomer did succeed in entering the compartment occupied by Moishe and his companions. He sat in astonished silence while the trebblers concluded their devotions, and then listened, bewildered, as they talked to each other in Yiddish. But Moishe had a kind heart, and he felt sorry for this lost soul sitting opposite him. He took down a brown paper parcel from the rack and extracted from it a huge sandwich of black bread and chopped herring. This he broke in two, and keeping half for himself he handed the other half to the fearful Gentile. 'Nem!' ('take!') he said kindly. The man's name was Mackenzie, and he was an insurance agent on his way to Burntisland: he later told the story to his friends in an Edinburgh bar. 'I ate for dear life,' he said. 'And, you know, it tasted damn good. Some kind of caviare.'

The anecdote I have just told was part of the Edinburgh Jewish folklore which grew up in the city in the first quarter of this century. I cannot vouch for its literal truth, any more than I can for the effectiveness of the trebblers' devotions in scaring away non-Jewish passengers. But these stories are all probable in the Aristotelian sense. I myself, on the one occasion when I went to Dundee on that train, saw the trebblers in their special compartments, a voluntary and jealously preserved segregation. Recently I received a letter from the son of the man who was stationmaster at one of the small railway stations where the earliest trebblers would alight; he told me how, at the very beginning of this century, these Jewish immigrants, not yet knowing any English, would converse with his father, they talking in Yiddish and he in broad Scots, with perfectly adequate mutual intelligibility. Scots-Yiddish as a working language must have been developing rapidly in the years immediately preceding the First World War. It must have been one of the most short-lived languages in the world. I should guess that 1912 to 1940 was the period of its flourishing. The younger generation, who grew up in the 1920s and 1930s, of course did not speak it, though they knew Yiddish; and while there is an occasional old man in Edinburgh who speaks it today, one has to seek it out in order to find it, and in another decade it will be gone for ever. 'Aye man, ich hob' getrebbelt mit de five o'clock train,' one trebbler would say to another. 'Vot time's yer barmitzvie, laddie?' I was once

asked. 'Ye'll hae a drap o' bramfen (whisky). It's Dzon Beck.
Ye ken: "Nem a schmeck fun Dzon Beck."' ('Take a peg of
John Begg', the advertising slogan of John Begg whisky.)
There was one word in the Scots-Yiddish vocabulary that
has always puzzled me: this was 'bleggage', applied to an
ill-behaved youngster. My father used to maintain that it was
a corruption of 'blackguard', and perhaps it was a mixture
of 'blackguard' and 'baggage'. Whatever its origin, it was
a fine, expressive word, and it was never more effectively
used than one sabbath morning in 1919 when a number of
enterprising youngsters had climbed on to the roof of the
Graham Street synagogue and were making a noise on the
skylight. The *chazan* (cantor) stopped his singing, banged
his large prayer book with the flat of his hand, and cried out:
'Shah! Mak a quietness! *Bleggages*!' This was just after my
father had accepted his appointment as Edinburgh rabbi,
and the incident was symbolic of the kind of chaos he was
determined to put a stop to.

We ourselves had little contact with what might be called
the trebbling stratum of Edinburgh Jews. We met them in
shul and saw them often enough in the streets of the city or at
Waverley Station, and we exchanged Scottish–Jewish funny
stories with their children, but my father's view of the nature
of a Scottish–Jewish community and its future development
as a separate but equal part of the culture within which it lived
left little room for these people. He got on well with them,
and looked after their religious needs, acting with respect
to them much more like the old-fashioned *rebbe* than like
the spiritual leader of Scottish Jewry, a public figure with
a dignified part to play in Scotland's capital, which was
his most impressive rôle. The trebblers combined Jewish
orthodoxy with superstition and were unable to distinguish
between central Jewish traditions and the flimsiest kind of
folklore. ('Shah! Iz nit mazel,' ['Be quiet! It's unlucky!']
one of the most patriarchal of the trebblers said angrily to
his wife when she started to offer me her condolences on the
death of my father.) Moishe Pinkinsky could be of no help to
my father in his ambition to reconcile rabbinic Judaism with

western secular culture. Moishe and his like were regarded in our family with affectionate indulgence as interesting examples of a transitional stage in the emancipation from the Ghetto.

I think now that they had more to offer than our aristocratic family attitude conceded. They had a folk wisdom of their own, and a tremendous emotional vitality in their way of living. I remember Motty Rifkind, a shambling, grizzled man, the elder of two extremely pious brothers. He sat next to me once in *shul* one Passover morning, and was indignant with some young men, infrequent visitors to the synagogue, who were chattering loudly throughout the *chazan's* repetition of the *Amidah* (an important prayer, with 'eighteen benedictions', which the congregation recite first, standing, and then the *chazan* repeats). As old Motty himself used the synagogue as if it were his club, sleeping, snoring, talking, arguing, or praying as the spirit moved him, I was a little surprised at his stern view of the talkers, and indicated as much. In reply he told me a story. 'Two men', he said, 'vent into a poob and ordered a glass beer. Dey hadna been in dat poob more dan vonce or tvice before. Vell, day sip deir beer un' dey sit talking un' *shmoosing* (chatting). Dey sit un' talk un' talk. At lest de barman leans over de counter und he says to dem: "Drink op yer beer. Get oot frae here. Ye coom into ma poob vonce a year un' ye tink ye can sit here un' *shmoos* for hours as do' ye owned de place. Ma regular customers can sit un' talk over deir beer as long as dey like. But no' you. Oot!" *Nu*, dat's hoo it is mit a *shul*, I come here every week und *Hakodosh boruch hu* ("the Holy One, blessed be He", that is God) kens me vell, un' he don't mind if I take it easy. But dese bleggages, dat come vonce or tvice a year — no! Dey *daven* (pray) or dey shot op.'

Another remarkable character, who spoke Scots–Yiddish though he was no trebbler, was the *shamosh* or beadle of the synagogue, a ginger-bearded gentleman, whom I shall call Schloimowitz, with a remarkable number of talents. He used to teach the elementary class in the *cheder* or Hebrew school and an extraordinarily effective teacher he was, too, though his methods would have horrified any modern educationist. He taught everything by simple repetition; the class would chant the words together over and over again in a sleepy, monotonous sing-song, until they knew them. I remember on summer evenings hearing the Hebrew chanting float out of the open windows of Sciennes School, a handsome grey stone public elementary school that stood at the top of our street, and wondering what the passers-by would think. (Incidentally, the fact that the *cheder* was conducted in one of the Edinburgh Education Authority's schools and no longer in the damp basement of the Graham Street synagogue was a characteristic achievement of my father's. He proved to the Edinburgh Corporation, or whoever was responsible, that the teaching of Hebrew to Jewish children in Edinburgh was an integral part of the city's educational activities, with the result that this school was put at his service, after ordinary school hours, free, and the *cheder* was able to move from its cramped and inadequate basement quarters.) Schloimowitz was extremely well up in Jewish customs and traditions, he knew to a nicety how to vary the tune of the chanting on the different holy days and at precisely what angle the feet should be kept while standing up to pray (the posture was modelled on the description of the angels praying in the book of Ezekiel) so that, although he had a voice that croaked like a raven's, he often acted as *chazan sheini* or second cantor. He also was in charge of a boys' service on Sunday mornings, where a different boy conducted the proceedings each week and so everyone learned the rather tricky process. Though my father sent Lionel and myself to Schloimowitz's service, for he felt we ought to know how to conduct a weekday service (something that every Jew is supposed to be able to do and may be called on to do as a mark of honour or sympathy), he was not very happy about it. He wanted us to learn all our religious and Hebrew knowledge from himself rather than from a character, however estimable, who had only half emerged from the Ghetto.

The living that Schloimowitz made from his activities as *shamosh*, Hebrew teacher, and extra cantor, he found far from adequate, and to eke out his income he engaged in a remarkable number of private enterprises. He would sell you anything. He specialised in obtaining articles required for Jewish worship, and he sold not only prayer books and praying shawls but Palestine wine and brandy and the palm branches and citrons used at the Feast of Tabernacles. He had no licence to sell wines and spirits, and his activities here were completely illegal; but nobody worried about that. Even my father, one of the most scrupulous men in the world where the law was concerned, would not hesitate to send me to Schloimowitz's house to ask for a bottle of 'oil', which was delivered wrapped up in layers of brown paper and marked 'frying oil' on the outside. Schloimowitz made a fair amount of money out of his various activities and eventually bought himself a handsome house in a residential area of the city. It was after he had moved there that he formed the habit of dropping in at a pub in Dalkeith Road for a small whisky or two. With his neatly trimmed beard and dignified bearing, he was taken by the barmaid and by the habitués of the pub for the rabbi, and I remember how horrified my father was when he learned this, especially at the detail that a certain brand of whisky had become known in this pub as 'the rabbi's choice'.

Schloimowitz liked his whisky, but he got drunk only once a year, and I have never seen a man set about it with more deliberation and dignity. It was on *Simchas Torah*, the feast of the Rejoicing of the Law, when one is supposed to have a merry time, that he would engage on this annual spree. There would always be a modest feast prepared in the synagogue hall after the morning service on *Simchas Torah*; glasses of wine for the young people and ladies, whisky for the maturer males, and biscuits. My father would stay to make *kiddush* (sanctification; that is, ask a blessing) over the wine, and then leave; but Lionel and I would linger on to watch Schloimowitz tanking up and to see what was going to happen. The climax was well worth waiting for. People would keep pressing glasses of whisky on him, and as he knocked them back in rapid succession (he had the extraordinary faculty, which I have seen in no one else, of being able to throw drink right down his gullet without any contraction of muscles for swallowing) his face would begin to glow redder and redder, and at length he would begin to address the company in Yiddish, making what was evidently an extremely funny speech of which I could never make out more than a few words. Then someone would clear a path between the glasses on the long trestle table: this was the signal for the grand finale. Up jumped Schloimowitz on to the table and, singing a song punctuated with frequent shouts and 'oi's', he moved down the table in a species of cossack dance, arms folded, knees bent, legs kicked out alternately. Never once did he knock over a glass. The whisky seemed to give him a curious kind of stability and control: the whole performance appeared to me superhuman. Up the long table he danced, then turned and danced back, singing and shouting, while the spectators clapped rhythmically. Then he jumped down, and the party was over. Lionel and I would hurry home, to be scolded for being late for dinner.

When I last saw Schloimowitz, not long ago, he was verging on 80, but looked as trim and spry as ever. My father, he told me, had worked too hard, and that had been the cause of his death. We were both silent for a moment and then he laughed and said: 'I never vork too hard, dat's vy I keep so vell. Vonce dey asked me to take an extra class at *cheder*. But I vasna having any. "Nae fear," I said.'

Scots-Yiddish was the language of those immigrant Edinburgh Jews who for the most part never managed to rise very high in the social or financial scale. It must not be confused with the more courtly though equally quaint broken English spoken by well-to-do immigrants who prospered in business. Notable among these (or perhaps he was really unique and I am constructing a class out of a single individual) was Mr Solomon Sklovsky, a somewhat deaf old man with a beautifully clean white beard and a fresh rosy face, who had made a fortune out of sugar. He had the reputation of complete probity combined with extreme cunning in the business world, and many stories were told of his shrewdness and enterprise. Thrift for him was the greatest of virtues ('Trift', he called it), and whenever an Edinburgh Jewish boy celebrated his *barmitzvah* he would open an account for him at the Savings Bank with a deposit of one pound. He was not fundamentally uncharitable by disposition, but he had to be persuaded of the complete worthiness of any cause before he would give a penny to it, and many a weary evening my father spent wrestling with him before extracting a promise to give a substantial sum to some Jewish or general charity. I think he enjoyed having to be persuaded, and was particularly pleased when a complete delegation waited on him; it gave him a sense of his own importance. He knew, too, that everyone waited to see how much Solomon Sklovsky ('Shlomo', he was called, the Hebrew for 'Solomon', and this became corrupted somehow to 'Shlabber') would give before deciding on his own contribution.

Old Shlabber lived in a world by himself. He was a widower when I first knew him, living alone with, I believe, a housekeeper of some sort to look after him. At the synagogue he would sit nodding his head and stroking his snowy beard, occasionally turning to his neighbour to roar out some observation or question. His deafness made him imagine that everyone else had to be shouted at, and once he startled me by roaring at me across several empty seats, during the Reading of the Law one Sabbath morning: 'De Hebrew lankvitch is de FINEST lankvitch in de vorlt.' He professed to scorn the younger business men who were coming to the fore in community affairs, and on one occasion, when the newly elected *parness* and *gabai* (president and treasurer) of the congregation took their seats for the first time in the special box appointed for them in the synagogue, he was heard muttering to himself as he eyed them: 'Fonny tink. VERY fonny tink.' His appearance was incredibly venerable; he was by far the most patriarchal looking of all the Edinburgh Jews. When, early in 1925, my father left from Waverley Station, Edinburgh, to go to Palestine for the opening of the Hebrew University in Jerusalem, Shlabber Sklovsky was among the group of senior members of his congregation who came to see him off. A photographer from one of the Edinburgh evening papers took a photograph of the scene, and that evening a picture of Shlabber appeared, with the caption: 'Dr Salis Daiches, Chief Rabbi (my father was often called Chief Rabbi though he had no such official title and always disclaimed it when it was given him), leaving Waverley Station, Edinburgh on his way to Jerusalem for the opening of the Hebrew University.' Obviously, the sub-editor or whoever it was who handled this item assumed that this venerable, patriarchal figure must be the rabbi, and cut out the rest of the photograph. My mother was most distressed when she saw this, and communicated with the newspaper, with the result that the next day a proper photograph of my father appeared, with a similar caption. But the damage had been done: my mother received some days later a puzzled letter from an old Liverpool friend whom she had not seen since the early years of her marriage, saying that she had seen the photograph of my father in the paper and she was upset to find how much he had aged, and indeed changed beyond recognition.

Shlabber's pronunciation of English was something quite original, and when combined with his characteristic roar made his speech unmistakable. I remember once answering the telephone when my father was out, with the ensuing conversation going something like this:

Myself: Hello?

Shlabber (*roaring*): Goot eefning Doctor Daiches!

Myself: I'm sorry, Mr Sklovsky, but Dr Daiches isn't in.

Shlabber: HA?

Myself: I'm sorry, Mr Sklovsky, but Dr Daiches isn't in.

Shlabber: HA? ?

Myself (*shouting*): I'm sorry, Mr Sklovsky, but Dr Daiches isn't in.

Shlabber (*roaring even louder than before, in a tone of absolute astonishment*): HOW DID YOU KNOW IT VOSS ME?

To the younger generation, these picturesque older men were the object of affectionate amusement. Some of the younger businessmen, born and bred in Edinburgh, were sometimes embarrassed when some of the more eccentric older characters appeared in the midst of a conversation with a non-Jewish colleague or customer. On one occasion, when a young Jewish rug-dealer in Edinburgh was interrupted in a talk with a titled Scottish customer by two bearded, Yiddish speaking collectors for a Jewish charity (one of them a bandy-legged red-headed man of incredibly slovenly appearance, who always wore, indoors and out, a too large bowler hat perched on the back of his head) he got rid of the intruders rapidly, then lightly remarked to the customer: 'Those are the Persians from whom I buy my rugs.' But on the whole there was little friction between different elements in the Jewish community or between the Jewish community and its non-Jewish neighbours. My father's success in welding the community into a single unit worshipping in the same synagogue had a great deal to do with this, while the Scottish Presbyterians' natural interest in the People of the Book helped to maintain good relations between Jews and Christians. Edinburgh University, for example, never made any difficulty about changing the dates of examinations when my father pointed out that they fell on Jewish festivals, and Jewish students would therefore be unable to take them; and on one occasion, when I was the only Jewish candidate, the professor sent the question paper to my father and asked him to see that I took the exam under the proper conditions. (My father stood outside the drawing-room door with his watch in his hand, and I never had to hand in a paper so punctually on the stroke of the hour as I had to on that occasion.) And before the war, when many Jewish students in America were finding it difficult to enter medical schools, my father arranged with the University of Edinburgh (and I think, but I am not positive, with the Royal College of Surgeons at Edinburgh as well) for the admission of a high proportion of American–Jewish students for that reason. There must be hundreds of Jewish doctors in America now who, though they have never realised it, owe their medical degree to the fact that my father intervened with the appropriate authorities to have them and their fellow citizens admitted at one or other of the two Edinburgh medical schools.

There are many other older Jewish characters who come to mind as I think of my childhood in Edinburgh. There is little Mr Lurie, who sat next to me in *shul*, who still greets me when I come back to Edinburgh and revisit the familiar synagogue with: '*Sholom aleichem* ('peace be with you'). Vell Davie howyer keepin?' 'Howyer keepin?', spoken in a peculiarly clipped accent, is the special way of greeting someone after long absence among these older Edinburgh Jews. Sometimes it is varied with, 'Keepin alright?' with a strong, upswinging interrogative inflection on the 'alright' (and sometimes an indeterminate vowel creeps its way in between the 'all' and the 'right'). There was Mr Solstone the tailor, dead many years now, whose beautiful new car (or was it his son's?) rolled backwards and fell over what he persisted in calling 'de barrication' beside Peebles Hydro. And I must not close these reminiscences without some mention of Yudel Simenoff, a man who combined extreme Jewish piety with Marxist orthodoxy and who, by reason of some palatal defect, was unable to speak his Scots-Yiddish dialect (for he, too, was one of the trebblers) without a whole battery of incidental spluttering noises. There were not more than half-a-dozen people in Edinburgh, outside his immediate family, who could understand him, and when he arose, as he unfailingly did, to make some remarks during the question period that followed the weekly lecture at the Edinburgh Jewish Literary Society, there were few if any who understood what he was talking about. Through hearing him often enough, I finally learned to understand him, and found to my surprise that he was in his way a learned and intelligent man, who knew a considerable amount about both Jewish folklore and folksong (his speech defect disappeared when he sang) and modern economics. In later life he began to write letters to the Edinburgh evening papers on economic and political affairs, and his opinions aroused respectful interest in many quarters. This was some twenty years ago, and when I was in Edinburgh soon after the war ended I did not expect to find him still flourishing. But I found that he had been discovered by the folklorists and had just been engaged to make some recordings of Jewish folksong and liturgical chants for the B.B.C. I realised then that somebody should have recorded the speech of Motty Rifkind and Moishe Pinkinsky in the 1920s and 1930s, the golden years of Scots–Yiddish. But nobody had thought of it then, and it was too late now.

CHAPTER EIGHT

My brother Lionel and I slept, throughout most of our childhood, in a large sparsely furnished room at the top of our three-storey house. It looked out across our own back garden to the back greens of the flats in Livingstone Place, where we could see housewives hanging up the clothes on washing day or at their windows, working by the sink. My bed was nearer the window, and it was my duty to open the window both top and bottom before settling down for the night. We both believed in fresh air, and the thought of sleeping with the windows shut — even in the dead of winter, and in an unheated room — would have horrified us. My father, however, had more old-fashioned notions on these matters. Every night, before going to bed himself, he would come up to our bedroom to make sure that all was well; he would close the bottom part of the window and pull out two of the three sections of shutter which were always built in (on the inside of the window) to serve as alternatives or supplements to blinds in older Edinburgh houses: the third, middle, section was hinged on to one of the other sections and folded behind it when the shutters were put back. Lionel and I would argue strenuously with our father about the question of window shutting; we insisted that we should suffocate if the bottom part of the window were closed, and my father protested that we would catch cold if it were left open. He had originally wanted to close both top and bottom and pull out all the shutters as well, but he reluctantly agreed to compromise by closing only the bottom window and leaving the middle section of shutter open, and eventually we allowed him to do this, though we kept on murmuring. We had our own way, at any rate, between the time of our going to bed and the time, generally a couple of hours later, when my father came up on his nightly visitation before going to bed himself. Sometimes, if Lionel or I woke up after my father had paid his nightly visit, the bottom of the window would be re-opened and the shutters folded back into the wall.

Neither of us had a bedside lamp, and the last one into bed had to pad across the cold linoleum to switch off the light by the door and then cross the room again in the dark. One winter Lionel, who was more enterprising than I was at that sort of thing, rigged up a complicated system of strings and pulleys which would enable either of us to put on or turn off the light without getting out of bed. It was fairly easy to rig up something which would switch the light on, but turning it off — which meant putting the switch *up*, and the switch was fairly high up on the wall — was a complicated matter to arrange, if it was to be done from a prone position. However, Lionel managed it, and the bedroom became a maze of strings running both horizontally and vertically. When my father came up the attic stairs that night to see that all was well and close the bottom part of the window, he ran inadvertently into this complicated machinery. He soon realised what it was for, and found to his dismay that he had dislocated an important part of the device so that the light could no longer be turned off from my bed. I was awake — I think the noise of his stumbling into the strings must have awakened me — and lay quietly watching. I thought he would have dismissed the whole thing as a silly prank, but to my surprise he looked genuinely distressed at finding that he had damaged the apparatus and immediately set about trying to repair it. My father was not deft with his fingers, and soon found himself in difficulties. He got down on the floor, he stretched towards the ceiling, he fiddled about with ends of strings, only to dislocate the machinery still further. Then he decided to remove all the strings and begin again from the beginning, working the thing out from first principles. Obviously, he didn't want us to be disappointed when we woke up in the morning. A rush of affection came over me as I watched him trying so hard and so vainly to restore the damage, and at last I could bear it no longer but jumped out of bed, exclaiming: 'It's all right. Don't bother. I can sort it.' ('Sort' is the common Edinburgh word for 'mend' or 'fix'.) My father watched rather sheepishly as I restored the apparatus to its original preposterous form, and then said: 'You'll catch cold. And why are you awake at this time of night?' There was no real reproof in his words, which were meant kindly, an attempt to establish communication. Indeed, his journey up to the top floor of the house each night before going to bed was itself a kindly and even sentimental gesture. But, though his life was full of such gestures, he found it difficult to put them spontaneously and informally into words. The most eloquent of men on formal, public occasions, he nevertheless found it hard to establish completely relaxed verbal communication with his children.

I fancy that he was like that, though in less degree, with my mother too. I remember once, for her birthday, he bought her a handbag more expensive than he could afford and handed it to her with an extraordinary *gauche* gesture. Neither he nor my mother knew what to say on the occasion: he was scolded for his extravagance. Years later, when I read Virginia Woolf's *Mrs Dalloway* and came across the incident where Richard Dalloway brings flowers home to his wife because he cannot find words to express what he wants to say, I thought I recognised the situation:

> But he wanted to come in holding something. Flowers? Yes, flowers, . . . The time comes when it can't be said; one's too shy to say it, . . . Here he was walking across London to say to Clarissa in so many words that he loved her. Which one never does say, he thought. Partly one's lazy; partly one's shy . . .

It was not laziness on my father's part, but a certain kind of shyness which seemed to overcome him in the simpler and more intimate affairs of life. Not that he lacked a robust sense of humour, or was incapable of joking with his family. He would listen tolerantly when Lionel or I vented our schoolboy humour at the dinner table, and would thoroughly enjoy our imitations of some of the more eccentric or picturesque members of his congregation. He was never in the least distressed when we engaged in somewhat boisterous fun during the *seder* night at the beginning of Passover, or when, on one occasion, I read to the assembled family and guests after the *seder* was over a would-be humorous parody of the service followed by a mystery story about a dubious Jewish preacher entitled 'Muffled in Matzo-meal, or the Mystery of the Meshugga Maggid (i.e. of the Mad Preacher)'. He had his own favourite jokes, too, and he would tell them with a roar of laughter which would sometimes go on until tears of mirth trickled down his cheeks and he was gasping for breath. I don't think I have ever known anybody with such a hearty laugh. He had also a somewhat academic fondness for the pun, and he would often make a punning remark at dinner and then look round the table with a smile for approval. (When he found grounds in his black coffee after dinner, he would look up and say, 'Grounds for complaint.' He must have made this remark a score of times, yet each time he expected the same approval.) But he was incapable of talking cheerfully affectionate nonsense to his family. His affection for and pride in us all was intense, but he could not express it easily in the give-and-take of daily conversation. When angered he could thunder at us most eloquently (we simply kept quiet and waited till the storm passed over), but mostly his talk was rather deliberate, rather formal.

I have, however, some very dim recollections of myself sitting on my father's knee as a very small child and being joggled up and down to the accompaniment of some nonsense verse (I seem to recall the phrase 'jingle-jangle-jorum') or of the verse:

Sandy Still belongs to the mill
And the mill belongs to Sandy still;
Sandy Still belongs to the mill
And the mill belongs to Sandy.

And once, in the pocket of a very old dress-coat of my father's that was brought forth from the dark recesses of some cupboard in a vast spring cleaning, we found a pair of white gloves (ladies'?) and a printed set of comic verses composed by him for his brother's wedding in (I think) 1905. The theme of the verses was the startling change about to take place in the state of both bride and groom: the chorus was the Latin tag, 'O quae mutatio rerum.'

When Lionel and I were students at Edinburgh University and would occasionally bring home a fellow student for tea, he would converse with him with a grave, old-world courtesy, always very punctilious about calling him *Mister* So-and-so, perhaps cracking a carefully prepared joke, talking about current affairs as though to an equal. Our university friends (who were mostly non-Jewish) were pleased and flattered by his manner and enjoyed talking with him. It is true that he occasionally got them mixed up, and was liable to say to Mr X, who was studying law, 'And you are the brilliant history student, aren't you?' — thinking of Mr Y, who had been to tea a few weeks before. But nobody seemed to mind that. And when he did learn what the student's main interest was, he would set out to make deliberate conversation on that topic. Once, I remember, he took a philosophy student into his study to chat with him about David Hume and Kant, and left me waiting outside, saying to myself ruefully that after all the visitor was *my* friend and had come to see *me*. The young man emerged thoroughly charmed.

My father never expected either Lionel or me to follow in his footsteps and take up the rabbinical profession, in spite of the fact that we came of a long line of rabbis stretching far back into the early Middle Ages and beyond, and we would be the first generation to break that tradition. It was clear from the beginning that Lionel had no ambitions that way; I went through a phase when I thought I should like to be a rabbi, but was very properly not taken seriously. Law was the subject my father's mind turned to when thinking of his sons' future. There is something about law which has always attracted the rabbinical mind, and my father himself, trained on talmudic argument, had considerable legal ability. My uncle, a rabbi and a distinguished biblical scholar and teacher of rabbinics in London, read law for amusement in his spare time and was called to the bar, though he hardly ever practised. So law was established in our family as a thoroughly suitable profession for a member of a rabbinical family. For Lionel, it was the obvious and proper choice; he had exactly the qualities of mind to make a good barrister (or advocate, as we say in Scotland). My own literary bent showed itself early, and I had no doubt myself of what I wanted to be. My father, though never discouraging my literary ambitions, at first assumed that I would want to go on and take a law degree after getting my honours degree in English at Edinburgh University. Literature, he thought, was an excellent thing as a second string. His attitude, in fact, was so similar to that of Robert Louis Stevenson's father to *his* son's literary ambitions (and, for that matter, to Walter Scott's father's attitude to his) that when I first read the life of Stevenson I was struck by the coincidence. (Indeed, the similarities between Stevenson's life and my own have often struck me since. Stevenson's problems as a young man in Edinburgh were startlingly like my own; his relations with his father were like mine; we both went to America for similar reasons; we both achieved the same kind of ultimate reconciliation with our families.) When I resisted the suggestion that I should proceed to a law degree after completing my degree in English, my father never brought the matter up again. I think he was impressed by my own confidence that I could make my way successfully in the literary profession. Most of the discussions on my career took place during my last year at school. When I entered the university and demonstrated how easy I found it to win distinction in literary courses, my father (who had not, I suspect, realised the possibilities of an academic career in literature before) seemed perfectly happy to let me go my own way. He boasted of my successes to his friends; and when I was elected Fellow of Balliol College, Oxford, he saw to it that the news was in the Edinburgh papers.

Life for my father had its duties and its courtesies, which he observed with what I can only call a scrupulous innocence. The subtleties of personal intercourse were left unspoken. It was the same with his attitude to religion. We all had our duties, which we were expected to fulful. We had to learn our Hebrew, attend *shul* regularly, wash our hands before eating and say grace afterwards, and (it went without saying) refrain from any of the activities offensive to an enlightened Jewish orthodoxy. Lionel and I would argue with our father about the reason for this or that Jewish observance, or even question its value or utility, but theology, or the mysteries of religion, or the nature of piety we never discussed with him. There was nothing of the mystic in my father, and his defence of Judaism (given often in addresses to literary societies and in articles in the press) was on the lines of a humanist utilitarianism: the good and useful and satisfying life was one led in accordance with laws and customs which safeguarded morality, preserved society, and decently canalised human instincts. The divine origin of such laws was a fact both manifested by Jewish history and required by human nature (for how could moral laws be absolute if they were not grounded in divine commands?). Yet his pulpit eloquence could reach to great emotional heights, and his magnificent sermons on *Yom Kippur*, the Day of Atonement, were full of deep religious feeling and a moving awareness of the ritual solemnity of communal repentance. I can see him now, rapt and prophetic in his white *kittel*, weak at the end of the day's fasting yet strong in voice and powerful in presence, leaning from the pulpit as he gives his final *Yom Kippur* sermon, his voice ringing out as he quotes and translates the Hebrew hymn beseeching forgiveness as the night falls and the day of penitence is coming to an end: 'Open unto us the gate, at the time of the closing of the gate, for the day fadeth.' I remember the *frisson* that used to go down my spine as I heard those words. Yet he would never take that tone in private conversation. It would have been unthinkable for him to talk to his family about sin or forgiveness or divine mercy. He would discuss with us the history of some law or custom, or the true meaning of some biblical text, or the short-sightedness of the 'Liberal' Jews in abandoning some traditional part of the liturgy or belittling the rabbinic tradition, but the ultimate truth of religion and the nature of religious experience were not for him topics of private conversation. After a day of religious exaltation and powerful preaching, he would return home on *Yom Kippur* night tired and relaxed to chat about the number of people in *shul*, decorum among the congregation, and the odd mumbling way in which old Mr Sklovsky had read *maftir Yonah* (i.e., the book of Jonah, which is read — or rather, chanted — by a distinguished member of the congregation at the conclusion of the afternoon Reading of the Law).

It may seem surprising that my father, who was so anxious to combine all that was best in modern thought with Jewish tradition and practice, should have been so opposed to Liberal Judaism (he himself rarely wrote that term without putting the first word in inverted commas), that modern Jewish movement whose aim is to concentrate on the finer ethical qualities of Judaism and prune away the element of tribal *tabu* (as they consider it) and rabbinical elaboration of minute prohibitions and observances. But in fact he was the implacable enemy of the movement. His synthesis combined orthodox, rabbinical Judaism with modern thought; to scrap every element of Jewish observance which modern thought would not accept was not to synthesise two different things but to tailor one to fit the other. And to tailor Judaism in that fashion meant substituting human claims to know what is good and right and to be able to distinguish the ethically valuable from the otiose for a belief in the divine origin of Jewish ethics. If the individual can go through the laws and practices which have developed in the course of Jewish tradition and say that some are still valuable and others are of no value and ought to be abandoned, then the individual is making himself the ultimate source of ethical absolutes, and saying that he will recognise as divine only what he, the individual, thinks is good. In his essay, 'Progressive Judaism: an Analysis', which appeared in his book, *Aspects of Judaism*, he quoted C.G. Montefiore's statement: 'Neither Hebrew Bible nor Rabbinic Talmud is immaculate or complete in doctrine or institution, in morality or in religion. We distinguish between the divine and human elements in both these books . . . We distinguish doctrines and institutions which we desire to maintain for their truth and their value from doctrines and institutions which we desire to put aside or to abolish.' And he commented: 'So it is "we", i.e. the exponents of Liberal Judaism, who are in possession of the unerring standards of truth, morality, and religion, and the application of these standards to the doctrines and institutions of Bible and Talmud enables these independent thinkers and moralists to decide for themselves what is true and what is false, what is valuable and what is valueless, what is permanent and what is transitory in the teaching and practices of Judaism.' He went on to develop his argument against Liberal Judaism as follows:

The obvious question that must occur to the thoughtful reader of such a pronouncement is this: Whence do the founders of the new faith derive those definite standards of 'truth', 'morality', and 'religion?' If these are not to be found in the religious teachings, but are to be applied to them; if the contents of the *Torah* (Law) are to be valued in accordance with principles fixed a *priori* or brought to bear upon them from other spheres; and if the critic is to pronounce his verdict in accordance with the estimate derived from those principles, must it not be asked whence these principles have themselves been derived? From what source does the 'Liberal' or 'Progressive' Jew draw his 'Truth', his 'Morality', his 'Religion', and how are these principles conveyed from one man to another? How are they imparted from teacher to pupil, from preacher to congregation? If the source is known and accessible, can it not be indicated, so that all may be able to test its purity and reliability? If it is a secret, when and how and to whom has it been revealed? If any man can discover these principles by his own reasoning power and his own moral postulates, why not leave it to every one to evolve his own faith and to fix his own religious principles — if he at all needs such additional safeguards and motives for right conduct? . . .

Again and again my father stressed the principle that unless we believe in the divine origin of the Law, human society is in perpetual jeopardy. 'There is scarcely an individual,' he wrote in his essay 'Modern Ethics and the Mosaic Law', 'or a body of individuals, that does nor feel entitled to take the law into his, or their, own hands when there is a chance of gaining some material advantage or profit. Is it not likely, therefore, that under the influence of the existing tendency, with positive religion losing its hold upon modern society, lawlessness and licence will increase, and the climax will one day be reached in a new upheaval, the greatest *bellum omnium contra omnes* that ever existed in reality — until from the chaos a new order of things will develop and humanity will have learned a new great lesson?' (This essay was written in the early 1920s.) Or again, even more explicitly: 'If the command, "Thou shalt love thy neighbour as thyself", or "Thou shalt not steal", or "Thou shalt not covet thy neighbour's house", etc., comes from God, the creator of man, the source of all truth and righteousness, and the omniscient and omnipotent guide of man's destiny — then it *must* be effective, then it *must* be obeyed by us, however much in our own opinion its transgression would be justified. To be religious means, in the words of Kant, "to recognize our duties as being divine commands." But while with Kant "divine commands" are nothing but dictates of man's own conscience, the average man will find that if the origin of those commands is not placed "in the starred heaven above us", his "moral conscience" will soon enough leave him in the lurch. This is the lesson which the modern ethicist has yet to learn.'

My father's chief objection to Liberal Judaism was thus that it made the individual conscience the arbiter of what was good and worth preserving and what was valueless and expendable in the law which had come down to us as the Word of God. Once you take that view, divine authority is gone and chaos is come again. My father would defend the Word of God most persuasively in humanist terms; he would show how obedience to it was conducive to a rich and satisfying personal and community life and how it was compatible with the best that all moral philosophers have said; but he would admit no argument about the reality of its divine origin. Historical or anthropological arguments about the Bible never disturbed him in the least: this was all very well, he would say in effect, but you *must* believe in the divine origin of the Law if society is to flourish. Once, when I was in the throes of hammering out my own position in relation to my father's, I accused him in my thoughts of really taking up Voltaire's position: 'If God did not exist it would be necessary to create him.' But that was unfair; he had a profound religious sensibility beneath the philosophical and humanist surface, though he was not always able to make articulate use of it.

I discuss this in some detail, because it explains how my father unwittingly destroyed for me in advance any line of defence to which I might retreat when I came to doubt the literal divine inspiration of the Bible and the talmudic tradition. The illogicality of the Liberal Jewish position was demonstrated for me once and for all. If the individual can pick and choose among the biblical precepts, saying that some sound rather attractive and worth keeping while others seem primitive and superstitious, then obviously the individual is creating God in accordance with his own ideas and the objectivity of religion disappears. Any kind of 'liberal' religion becomes a humane agnosticism using some of the forms of religion to find acceptance for its ethical views. It was a sad irony of fate that made my father's earnest and eloquent crusade against Liberal Judaism point the way to agnosticism for me; but in some sense that is what happened.

My father in his innocence took much for granted. Most of all, he took for granted that the deep, unmentioned roots of his own faith would spread automatically down the generations. He, as an orthodox Jewish rabbi and a student of Hume and Kant, had finally solved the relation between Judaism and modern secular culture and showed how one could be a free and equal citizen of a western democracy while keeping up all orthodox Jewish observances: there was nothing for Lionel and myself to do but to follow in his footsteps. Though he never thought of us as becoming rabbis, I don't think that it once crossed his mind that we would ever question his synthesis, and throughout our childhood the pattern of family loyalties and family affection was woven so closely and strongly that any such questioning was unthinkable. Even when as a child I wondered about the existence of God, it never occurred to me to wonder about my father's British–Jewish way of life. And I was troubled about the existence of God. For some time in my childhood the only concrete proof I could find was that people did not have children until they were married: this, I argued, showed clearly that God really did preside over human affairs and took care to send children to couples after marriage. But when I discovered that birth was a biological process that was possible without marriage, I realised at once that the only tangible proof of God's intervention in human affairs had been removed. Night after night, on going to bed, I used to plead with God to send me that night some sign to prove His existence — some dream, some token, however slight, that would indicate that He was there and had heard me. None ever came. This was not the kind of thing I could discuss with my father.

As I grew older, and became interested in Jewish history and the whole fascinating process of the development of Jewish tradition, I accepted Jewish orthodoxy and my father's synthesis out of pride in the Jewish cultural heritage, and was less bothered about the existence of God. I came to see the theological questions as subordinate to the more practical question of the basis of a culture. There was a period in my teens when, passionately devoted to the Zionist cause, I saw myself in a Messianic rôle leading the Jewish people back to their ancient homeland. And I remember during my first year at Edinburgh University thinking that the summit of my academic ambitions would be to become Professor of English at the newly founded Hebrew University in Jerusalem. It is perhaps a sad and certainly an ironic comment on human affairs that when I was offered that position at the end of the war I declined it.

The change which resulted in my life when I left school and entered Edinburgh University was enormous, and had far-reaching consequences. At school I had done my work and gone home, taking no part in sports or other extra-curricular activities. But the university was different. There was a great variety of social and intellectual life outside the lecture room, and it was not mostly confined, as non-academic school activities were, to Friday night and Saturday; I found myself joining societies, writing for the student magazine, making friends among my non-Jewish fellow students. I discovered, to my delighted astonishment, that my fluency in speech and facility in turning verse, which had helped to amuse the family at home but which I had not till now thought to be in any degree out-of-the-way qualities, made me a popular and sought-after figure at the university, and Lionel, too, found that his oratorical gifts and genius as a *raconteur* gave him an important place in student life. I remember, after taking part in the annual Associated Societies Debate early in my undergraduate career, I was congratulated by the chairman, who remarked: 'I suppose at school you must have run the Literary and Debating Society single handed.' I merely smiled in reply: I did not like to tell him that at school I was never able to attend the Literary and Debating Society because it met on Friday nights, nor did I admit that this was my first appearance at a public debate. In due course I became Senior President of the English Literature Society, Junior President of the Diagnostic Society, and literary editor of *The Student*. I found myself being continually surprised that I was actually taking a prominent part in such activities.

The sense of liberation was intoxicating. I had not realised before how narrow and indeed lonely my life had previously been. There was, of course, the family circle with its loyalties and affections; but in my last years at school, when my literary interests were growing and I was going through a phase of romantic introspection, I had no one to discuss these things with, and got into the habit of going for long walks alone. I even grew for a while apart from Lionel, with whom I had grown up in closest association, for as we became older our interests came to differ. And I had no close friends at school — at least none of whom I saw anything outside school hours. But now I was free of a new and richer world, and not only free of it but sought after by it.

At first this had no effect on my Jewish feeling. I was, in fact, aggressively Jewish, taking every opportunity of pointing out my background and, I am afraid, rather snobbishly insisting on its superiority. When, in my first year at the university, I fell sentimentally in love with a fellow student (it was an extraordinary calf-love affair: I had hardly spoken to a girl except my sisters before that) we exchanged passionate avowals and then decided to part for ever because my being Jewish made any further relationship impossible. (The decision, I should add, was mine, not hers. It never occurred to *her* that there was a barrier.) I had a broken heart for almost a year after that. I also did some serious thinking. To my father, it was inconceivable that I should even take a non-Jewish girl out to tea. Indeed, it was inconceivable to him that Lionel or I should take *any* girl, even one of deep Jewish orthodoxy, out to tea or anywhere else. The Daiches boys didn't do that. We were the rabbi's sons, and known, and we were not to be seen going about with a girl. When the time came, we would be introduced to beautiful, intelligent and perhaps also wealthy Jewish girls from cities which had larger Jewish populations than Edinburgh, and we would then doubtless fall in love and get married. Or, if we did not fall in love with the first one provided, there would be others. Here again, my father's innocence was shattering. He was bitterly angry as well as puzzled when he once met Lionel walking with an extremely respectable Jewish girl in an Edinburgh street. This was when I was having my first romantic love affair with the non-Jewish student, and it occurred to me that if my father felt this way when Lionel went for a walk with a Jewish girl from an orthodox family, what would he have said had he known that every day I had been walking my girl home from the university?

Oddly enough, my father never made any objection to our going to university dances, whatever his private misgivings might have been. But it was unthinkable that we should take a girl to a dance we attended; we went alone, or as a member of a large party where the couples were not paired off. What my father thought we did at these dances I cannot imagine. The difficulty, if not the sheer impossibility, of going to a dance alone never seems to have occurred to him. Lionel, always more enterprising than I was in these matters, once arranged to take to a university dance the daughter of a highly respected member of the Edinburgh Jewish community. When my father found out that he intended to take this girl to the dance, he was thunderstruck. An enormous storm broke, and the upshot was that Lionel went to the dance alone. Fortunately, he went in his capacity as business manager of the university society that was running the dance, so he had an excuse for breezing in by himself, as though to see how things were going.

Deceit was forced on me by degrees. My father knew that I was a member of several university societies attended by both sexes. He knew that girls attended the university lectures. Presumably it was all right if I got into conversation with a girl after a lecture or after a society meeting. Was it all right to walk a few steps while talking with her? If so, how many? The position was, in fact, ludicrous. I began to ask myself whether this 'So far and no further' attitude between Jews and non-Jews was healthy or desirable or even, over any length of time, possible. And when I found that I made friends at the university to whom I could talk

more freely and satisfyingly than to any Jewish friends or
relations, the problem became more acute still. No one
had warned me of the possibility that I might find some
non-Jews more *sympathique* than any Jews I knew. This
was a most disturbing revelation to me, and it made
toeing the invisible line imposed by the policy of Jewish
self-segregation not only physically almost impossible but
a great strain psychologically. It was all very well for my
father to speak to enthusiastic Gentile audiences at Burns
clubs or anti-Hitler protest meetings; he was a rabbi, with
his status, his mission, his publicly recognised position
as a Jewish leader. My position was very different: I was
exploring friendship for the first time in my life, and I found
the invisible line increasingly illogical. The first time that
I took a girl to a dance was at the end of my first year
at the university when, secretly and with every kind of
precaution against being found out at home, I took the
fellow student I was in love with. (Let the psychologists
say what they like about the sense of guilt, but the fact is
I had a wonderful time. I was a poor dancer; most of the
time we sat in a corner and talked.) The second time was
some years later, when I had matured considerably both
intellectually and emotionally; I took then another fellow
student, who was to become my wife.

Thus it was that a policy of anguished reconsideration
of the relation between my Jewish background and my
non-Jewish environment was forced on me. It was a long,
difficult and painful process, which was not complete until
the end of my years as a research student at Oxford. My
deep affection and admiration for my father never altered,
but I had a sense of living on the edge of a precipice. I
would come home from a walk on the Pentlands with a
group of my university friends (or with only one of them),
to find, say, preparations for Passover in progress, and I
would feel as though I was walking from one century into
another. My non-Jewish friends made things as easy for me
as they could. They knew I ate no meat at their houses; they
knew that Friday night and Saturday were impossible times

for me; when I was asked to take part in a play put on by one of the university societies, the performance was arranged for the evenings of Tuesday, Wednesday and Thursday instead of the usual Thursday, Friday and Saturday. But though this saved me inconvenience it only increased my sense of living in two worlds, and sometimes in an abyss between them. I remember particularly one winter evening coming from a convivial meeting of a university society to a Friday night service at the synagogue. There was only a handful of people, old men mostly, at the service, and as the slow and melancholy notes of the concluding hymn *Yigdal* rose thinly up to the roof, I thought of the centuries during which this hymn had been sung, of long dead Jewish congregations in Provence, the Rhineland and Poland, who had held so steadfastly to their Jewish way of life and passed their heritage unchanged on to their children. I thought of the long roll of Jewish martyrs, those who had given their lives for 'the sanctification of the Name'. I thought of my own ancestors, of my grandfather and of *his* father, Aryeh Zvi Daiches, whose picture I had seen on the wall of my grandfather's study, a noble looking man in a fur-trimmed cap, one of the innumerable Jewish scholars and teachers from whom I was descended.

My affection for my father increased, if possible, as I realised how innocent and how vulnerable he was. At the same time, I read Jewish apologetics with an increasingly critical eye. I re-read my father's *Aspects of Judaism*, noting in the margin arguments which I could not find convincing. I studied the Jewish prayer book, and noted the difference between the strains of noble piety and crude superstition. I came to see the Hebrew Bible as a fascinating record of the spiritual development of a people rather than as a book of conduct inspired by God. When I went to Oxford, and engaged in research on English translations of the Hebrew Bible, I pursued my Hebrew studies and read more and more about biblical history and about the development of Judaism. I read much Zionist literature, as well as modern Hebrew poetry. I translated some of the poems of Jehudah

Halevi into Scots. Unconsciously, I was preparing for a showdown with my father. Whatever happened, I was not to be accused of lack of knowledge of or affection for my ancestral heritage.

All the time I was at Oxford I was wrestling with the problem of reconciling my deep love for my parents, and my persisting affection for the Jewish traditions with which I was brought up, with the psychological realities of my present situation. Night after night I lay awake conducting imaginary dialogues with my father. I was profoundly in love with my former fellow student at Edinburgh, and though I had never formally proposed we both knew that sooner or later we must and would marry. (And let me at this point give the lie direct to those who claim that inter-marriage never works: I write within a month of our eighteenth wedding anniversary, and I know of few marriages which have been as consistently happy and mutually rewarding as ours.) At the same time I was, of my own choice, conducting the services at the somewhat makeshift Jewish synagogue in Oxford, and writing my weekly letters to my father in Hebrew. It was not a happy time, and though of course I remember many individual happy occasions at Oxford it is hardly an exaggeration, though it sounds melodramatic, to say that my years there were blighted by the nightmarish situation in which I found myself.

Showdowns between different generations are never really possible, and I learned that, too, eventually. True, my father was innocent and vulnerable; but he had his own dignity and his own sense of responsibility towards his congregation. There was a point at which argument failed, and he fell back on that dignity and that responsibility. For all our clannishness and profound mutual affection and loyalty, we were not a demonstrative family. Only at the moment of bitterest difference between my father and myself did he bring himself to voice sentiments of tenderness and of love. Not long afterwards, when I was on my way to America with my wife, a radiogram was brought to me as I lay, slightly sea sick, on my bunk. It was from my father and mother, and read: 'Yom Kippur blessings.' It was the Day of Atonement, 1937.

I accepted an academic position in America, at the University of Chicago, purely for my father's sake. I went there so that he would not feel embarrassed (or even, as he once desperately suggested, compelled to resign his position as rabbi in Edinburgh) by anything that I had done or would do. I had at that time no particular interest in America, nor was I at all anxious to go there: I resigned my fellowship at Balliol with reluctance. Yet of course there was the sense of high adventure and, more important, the knowledge that I was sharing that adventure, that my wife and I were starting out for the New World together. Once there, we had an orthodox Jewish marriage for my father's sake, and looked forward to returning permanently to Britain after a few years. As it happened, though we came home for a visit in 1939, the war kept us in America for many years more. They were in many respects happy and fruitful years, and we made firm friends there. But we felt ourselves, particularly during the war, to be exiles, cut off from the country and the people that claimed our deepest attachment. I was horrified when one of my former teachers at Edinburgh wrote to me in America applauding my decision to 'get out while the going was good'. I pestered the British consular authorities in Chicago for advice on how to get back, and, when a scheme was introduced facilitating the voluntary return of British subjects residing abroad provided they would join one of the services on arrival, I signed up at once, stipulating only that my wife and two children should be given transportation back with me, for otherwise I would be unable to support them. While waiting for transportation I was given a position with British Information Services in New York, and after a while I was requisitioned by the British Embassy in Washington, where I remained (except for two official visits back to England) until 1946. By that time I had long since lost my place in the academic queue in England, and was glad to accept an attractive offer from Cornell, where we remained for five years before a suitable academic opening in England made our permanent return possible. My American friends will think this an ungenerous and perhaps even an inaccurate account of my feelings towards my long American sojourn. They know how easily and happily my wife and I fitted in to the American academic communities where I worked. Yet always we talked and planned of coming home. We lived on two levels, as it were, the immediate present, busily and happily in America, and the deeper nostalgic level, which we revealed only to each other.

If I were writing a novel based on my own life it would end with the summer of 1939, when my wife and I, with our small son, came home to the happy ending that I had always profoundly believed in. We took a cottage in Perthshire by the River Tay for the summer months, while I did some writing. My father and mother made inquiries and found a nearby farmhouse to let for August, so they spent August there, just across the river from us. Part of that time my wife's people were with us too (and how tactful and understanding they had been throughout the whole affair!). We would go over to the farmhouse on Friday night, for the traditional sabbath eve dinner. Somehow an inclusive world had been established, which took us all in. Arguments, I knew now, were futile and cruel. I remember a sunny afternoon in the garden of our cottage, with my parents leaning over their grandson in his pram. It was about ten days before the beginning of the Second World War.

The last scene of all was in December, 1944. I was working in the British Embassy in Washington, and had been flown over to Britain to spend some time at the Ministry of Information in London. I managed to get a week's leave in Edinburgh. I had not seen my parents since that summer in 1939, a time that now seemed worlds away. As the taxi stopped outside the familiar house — shabbier than I remembered it, but otherwise startlingly the same — I found it hard to believe that this was me, returning, in 1944. The front door was open and I went in, and there in the drawing-room, huddled over a small electric heater, were my father and mother. It was a bitterly cold day, and coal was in short supply. My father had his arm in a plaster cast, and I learned that he was recovering from a nasty accident. I sat between him and Mother, and we talked.

My father's arm mended steadily, and the following Saturday he insisted (against all advice) on going to *shul* and preaching. I went with him, holding his arm so that he would not slip on the icy pavement. I looked frail and worn as he stood in the pulpit to begin his sermon, but his voice was as strong as ever. His *talith* kept slipping off his shoulders, and, as he had only the use of one arm, he was unable to put it back: I had to go up and help him. He took as his text the account (from that day's portion of the Law) of Jacob sending young Joseph to seek his brothers in Shechem, and went on to discuss the whole question of youth going out beyond the ken of the older generation. Why should Jacob have allowed his beloved young son to go out into the dangers which he knew were awaiting him? Was not this being a bad father? No; Jacob was right. There is a point beyond which a parent cannot be protective towards his children, and Jewish parents often err through not realising this. Jacob was right in sending his rather pampered young son into dangers away from home: Joseph would have to work out his own salvation. And perhaps the older generation can learn from the younger. I think he was speaking to me, offering fuller understanding and reconciliation. But, as always, he was more at home in public than in private utterance. A handful of regular attenders, a few American–Jewish soldiers, a couple of R.A.F. boys on leave, heard my father's last testament: but he and I knew for whom it was meant.

I left Edinburgh the next day: 'It won't be five years before I am back again to see you next time,' I said to my father on departing. But I never saw him again. Though I did not know it at the time, he was in fact dying of a disease he had long concealed from everybody. If he had gone into hospital for appropriate treatment in time, he could have been cured easily. But he hated the idea of a deputy doing his work; this was his congregation, he had welded it together, and he would minister to it until the end. And he did. After his accident he continued to preach regularly, attend meetings, deliver public speeches, and carry on all his multifarious duties as rabbi, until, some five months later, he collapsed one evening after a day crowded with meetings and died shortly afterwards.

None of his children was with him when he died. Lionel was in the army in Italy; Sylvia was on a war job in London; Beryl was on war service with the w.a.a.f.; I was in Washington. Only my mother sat by his bedside at the end. 'If only I had five more years,' he said to her when he realised he was dying; 'there is still so much to do.' He repeated, literally with his very last breath, the profession that a dying Jew traditionally makes of his faith: *Adonai hu ha-Elohim*, 'the Lord is God'.

I received the cable announcing his death before the arrival of the letters telling me of his illness. And a week afterwards I received a letter from my father himself (transatlantic mails could be very slow in war time); it had been written a few days before his final collapse. He spoke cheerfully of his regaining use of his 'strong right arm', and congratulated me on my promotion to a more responsible position at the Embassy. Months later, when I was in Edinburgh again, I was told by a member of my father's congregation who had visited him two days before his death that one of the first things my father had said to him was: 'David has got a fine new position at the British Embassy in Washington.'

* * *

Many times since his death people have suggested to me that I should write something about my father, or edit his sermons, or collect his essays and letters. But his sermons and his essays are not important in themselves: it was his personality that gave them life. He was a great preacher, but not a great sermon writer: his life was greater than his works. Indeed, his life *was* his work, and to separate the two is to do both an injustice. It is not my father's philosophy, his dialectical skill or his religious thought that was remarkable. His letters to *The Scotsman* divorced from the context of the particular occasion that prompted them have no especial interest today. These things are part of his biography, and must not be separated from it. But again, the mere facts of my father's life are of no importance. In any case, I know only a few of them. I do know my own life, however, and in telling part of that story I can tell all I know about my father. Once, asked whether he believed in personal immortality (a question on which I do not believe he ever committed himself), he smiled and said that one lives most effectively after death in the memories of those whom one has loved and taught. He was right: these chapters from my autobiography turn out to be a tribute to him. He is the hero, not I. And if this means that the story is a tragedy, he would not have flinched from that. The tragic hero, said Aristotle, has his *hamartia*, his flaw; but he is also a person of some stature and nobility.

Yet the story is tragic only if we read it too literally. True, my father's synthesis, however brilliantly illustrated in his own life, proved incapable of transmission to his children, at least in the form he gave it. His ultimate recognition of this was perhaps rueful rather than either complacent or tragic. But he went on with his ministry to the end, pursuing his chosen way of life with heroic dignity. The last thing he wrote was a series of charming essays for young people on the Jewish festivals. Perhaps, in talmudic phrase, his works exceeded his wisdom; his life is more memorable than his writings. And Rabbi Eleazar the son of Azaryah said that he whose wisdom exceeds his works is like a tree with many branches and few roots, easily overturned by the wind, while he whose works exceed his wisdom is like a tree with few branches and many roots, which cannot be overturned by all the winds that blow.

PROMISED LANDS
A Portrait of my Father

✡

Foreword

Over forty years ago I wrote, in *Two Worlds*, an account of my childhood in which I painted a portrait of my father as seen through my young eyes. His story and character have seemed to many people so interesting that I have been persuaded to attempt a direct portrait of him, drawing not only on my own memory of him but also on the memories of others, his own works, and my knowledge of relevant social and intellectual history. Though my imagination has also played some part in this picture, there is no detail in it that cannot be supported by something I know my father did, wrote or said.

David Daiches
Edinburgh, December 1996

I

The train from Newcastle steamed into platform 10 of Waverley Station and stopped, the engine emitting a loud hissing noise. The rabbi, who had been collecting small luggage from the overhead rack for the last few minutes, opened the carriage door and looked out. 'Here we are,' he said. 'Edinburgh, the capital of Scotland.' 'Come on, children,' said his wife to the three youngsters — two boys, one of eight years and one of six, and a girl just turned five — 'and don't forget anything.' They stepped out of the train into the fading winter light of an Edinburgh February afternoon in 1919. There on the platform was a delegation from the Edinburgh Hebrew Congregation waiting to welcome their new rabbi.

The family had come from Sunderland, changing trains at Newcastle. All were excited. They had lived for over ten years in Sunderland, where the rabbi had been the spiritual leader — he liked that phrase — of the Jewish community there. Now, having received a call from the Jews of Edinburgh, he was arriving with a sense of the fulfilment of a long-cherished hope. This was the city of the great eighteenth-century Scottish thinkers, of David Hume, on whom he had written his doctoral dissertation at Berlin and Leipzig. This was the home of Enlightenment, of that calm, rational approach to the knowledge of man and his environment that it was his mission to reconcile with the values and practices of rabbinical Judaism. He was elated. The children were eager and curious. Their

161

mother was somewhat worried: she did not know what
the future held. But the rabbi knew.

In the few seconds before he was approached and greeted
by the waiting delegation he was aware of the long journey he
had made. He saw himself as a small boy in Vilna, where he
had been born almost exactly thirty-nine years before, then as
a schoolboy in the little Jewish town of Neustadt–Scherwindt
where his father had been rabbi and head of the rabbinical
college. Studying Talmud with his father from the age of
five, tutored, along with his elder brother, by a gentile scholar
specially hired to teach the rudiments of western culture,
then a schoolboy across the border from Neustadt at the
Königsberg *Gymnasium* in East Prussia, then as a young
man studying rabbinics at the Hildesheimer rabbinical
seminar in Berlin and simultaneously studying philosophy
at the university — what a complex cultural journey he
had made. And now he was a respected rabbi as well as
an authority on David Hume, a Polish–Lithuanian Jew,
born into a Yiddish-speaking culture, who had moved to
a German environment and total fluency in the German
language, finally to fall in love with a sceptical philosopher
from distant Scotland and with the English language, which
he mastered with an ease that surprised himself.

Hume was the bridge. It was Hume who brought him
to work in the reading-room of the British Museum and
eventually to relinquish his Polish–Lithuanian–German
background to become a British citizen. He spoke English
with no trace of a foreign accent, but a little more formally
than any native of the British Isles, an English with an
eighteenth-century flavour, an English that marked his
final break with the Yiddish-speaking *golus* and a re-birth
into a promising world of cultural pluralism with which
his Jewish traditions could be comfortably domiciled.
He shook hands with the President of the Edinburgh
Hebrew Congregation and then with the other members
of the welcoming delegation. '*Boruch ha-bo*. Welcome to
Edinburgh.'

The porter, having collected it from the luggage van,

wheeled the family's abundant luggage, conspicuous among which was a large black trunk with a curved top on which were painted the rabbi's initials in white, and brought it to the cab rank. Two horse cabs had been commandeered to take the rabbi and his family together with the President of the Congregation (at whose house the family would be staying until they found a house of their own). There were taxis now, but some horse cabs remained, and it was fitting that the rabbi's entry into his long admired Edinburgh should be in that older form of conveyance. There flitted into his head a silly rhyme he had known as a boy (it emerged in English, though he had known it in Yiddish). *Yoshke took a droshky and went to Mosky.* Yoshke (a familiar diminutive of Joshua) was the popular Jewish name for Jesus, and the rhyme was a good-humoured anti-Christian joke.

But the rabbi was not an anti-Christian. He was — though the term was not then in use — a cultural pluralist, who believed in the comfortable co-existence of what he termed the 'higher' religions. Let each maintain its own traditions and not poach on any other's preserve. He deplored the activities of missionaries unless they concerned themselves with restoring the faith of their own people.

The ideal of the Hildesheimer seminary, from which he had won a distinguished *smicha* or rabbinical diploma (he also had one from his father and another from a famous Polish rabbinical scholar), was *torah im derech eretz*, which could be freely translated to mean 'Jewish religion and tradition together with the secular culture of the western world'. This was a German–Jewish invention, deriving ultimately from a Jewish response to the eighteenth-century Enlightenment as articulated by Moses Mendelssohn, on whom the rabbi had written an essay. Moses' grandson, Felix the composer, was not Jewish, since his own father had converted to Christianity. But the rabbi did not consider this as challenging the Hildesheimer synthesis.

His own father, a distinguished authority on the Jerusalem

Talmud (to be distinguished from the better known Baby-lonian Talmud), descendant of a long line of rabbinical scholars claiming among their ancestors great figures such as Rashi and Judah ha-Nasi and ultimately King David himself, while anxious to see his sons educated in western culture, was uncompromising in his insistence on their acquiring talmudic learning and maintaining the traditions of rabbinical Judaism. He was a product of the Yiddish-speaking *shtetl*, yet in his way he had looked outwards and made gestures to the modern world that (to the horror of the ultra-orthodox) had included sending his sons to a non-Jewish *Gymnasium*. He observed with pride that his sons could quote Homer in Greek and Virgil in Latin, but most of all that they were fluent in Hebrew and when they were away from home wrote all their letters to their parents in that language.

The rabbi was annoyed with himself when that silly little rhyme about Yoshke came into his head in the cab. It was part of a background of Yiddish folklore that he preferred to forget. His German education had led him to regard Yiddish (which was his native tongue) as an uncouth dialect of German. When he had to speak it, in talking with immigrant members of his congregation or in giving the occasional *droshe* or Yiddish sermon expected by such members, he used a highly Germanised form of the language. (A learned visiting Indian once compared it to Nehru's highly Sanskritised Hindi.)

Not for the rabbi the life of the *shtetl*. Not for him the stories of Sholem Aleichem or tales of the Chassidim. Not for him tales of the miracle-working *rebbe* or the folklore of the ghetto. *Torah im derech eretz*. The Torah was in Hebrew, not in Yiddish: Hebrew was the true Jewish language. He shared with Renaissance biblical scholars the view that Hebrew, Greek and Latin were the basic languages of western civilisation.

His father, in spite of his gestures towards the modern world, held no such view. But it was observed with uneasiness by his fellow Jews in Neustadt that he wore patent-leather shoes and that between *minchah* and *maarev* (the afternoon and evening services in the synagogue) he would walk along the street with a Christian official and talk in *Russian*. And though he otherwise always spoke Yiddish, he wrote only in Hebrew. He founded and edited a Hebrew magazine to encourage the use of the language.

The new Edinburgh rabbi thought of all this as the cab clattered along Princes Street and up Lothian Road. He had visited his father in Leeds just before coming north from Sunderland: he wanted to see him before taking up his new appointment. He had a close relationship with his father and had contributed a sermon (in Hebrew) to a published collection of the older rabbi's Hebrew discourses and commentaries. The rabbi had thought of Leeds as he sat in the train puffing northwards from Durham. His father's house there was purely East European Jewish in atmosphere, ritual, cuisine and language; his father lived in a Yiddish enclave in this English textile city ministering as rabbi to a congregation of mostly immigrant Jews. Patent-leather shoes and inter-service chats with gentiles notwithstanding, the older rabbi had no intention of assimilating in any way to an English environment. The younger rabbi reflected on the freaks of history that had brought his father to England. 'And because of our sins we were exiled from our land,' they recited in the *musaph* service of *Rosh Hashanah* and *Yom Kippur*, and what peregrinations that exile had provoked! He thought of his ancestors in ancient Israel, of King David and King Solomon and the subsequently divided kingdom, of the great Hebrew prophets, especially his favourite Isaiah whose marvellous rhetorical poetry stayed in his mind together with the sounding Greek of Homer and Virgil's plangent voice. From the Land of Israel where had they gone? They had been in the south of France, in the Rhineland, in Holland, Russia, Poland, Lithuania. And he had himself come from Germany to England, thence at last to the heavenly city of the eighteenth-century philosophers, Edinburgh. And now here he was. This is where he wanted to be.

His father, however — he reflected on this with some sadness as the cab rattled along Brougham Place towards the Meadows — had not wanted to be in Leeds. He had not been anxious to accept the invitation repeatedly extended to him by the Beth Hamedrash Hagadol in Leeds to come over and be their rabbi. But his hand had been forced by a strange circumstance, in which his son saw perhaps the hand of God. Many years before, the older rabbi and his wife had had a son who died in infancy. Through some confusion or negligence, his death was never officially registered. On the eighteenth birthday of the dead boy the Russian authorities (for all Poland and Lithuania was at this time part of the Russian Empire) called him up for military service. When the rabbi protested that the boy had died in infancy, the authorities refused to believe him, thinking that the parents were concealing the boy to prevent his being conscripted into the Russian army. To bring pressure on the rabbi they threatened to withdraw his official government licence to practise as a Jewish religious leader (then necessary throughout the Russian Empire before anyone could accept a rabbinical appointment). In the circumstances, he reluctantly accepted the invitation from Leeds. In the autobiographical preface to one of his Hebrew works he told the whole story, quoting the eloquent pleas of his congregation to stay with him as their guide and teacher, explaining how he left for England with a heavy heart. But his son was now arriving in Scotland with cheerful heart and high hopes. Two voyages, he thought, so similar and yet so different.

He had made two earlier journeys to the West. The first was to the Königsberg *Gymnasium*, where he mingled with German schoolboys in studying a western classical curriculum. But on winter Friday afternoons, when it grew dark early and the sabbath commenced, he had permission to lay down his pen and cease writing, for writing was not permissible on the Jewish sabbath. This Jewish youngster from the *shtetl* across the border was allowed to exercise his right to refrain from writing on the sabbath eve, even in a German high school. What enlightened times he lived in!

It had been a great adventure going to the university in Berlin, even if simultaneously he had been enrolled in the Hildesheimer rabbinical seminary. Western philosophy and Jewish rabbinical scholarship pursued simultaneously: that was Enlightenment for you! He and his elder brother, who simultaneously studied at the university and the seminary, took lodgings with a Berlin Jewish widow, and had their evening meal at the back premises of a kosher butcher's. It was rather disgusting, the rabbi later reflected, eating meat, however kosher, in the proximity of dead animals hanging on hooks and chopped-up carcases. But the meat he ate was kosher, and inexpensive.

The German student *mystique* of sodalities and duelling played no part in his student life in Berlin or later at Leipzig where, under the German system of *Lehrfreiheit*, he went to continue his philosophical studies under the great Paulsen. But he made some non-Jewish friends, discussed religion and philosophy with them, and enjoyed his glass of beer without inquiring too curiously into the ritual propriety of its production. Standing on the station at Newcastle awaiting the train to Edinburgh, he had noticed a penny-in-the-slot chocolate machine, and he remembered how on German railway stations there were coin-operated beer machines at which one could — and did — obtain a glass of beer for a trifling sum. That was another world. Although the world of Berlin high fashion was never his, he did acquire a dress-suit and a white tie, and very occasionally went all dressed up with friends to the theatre or concert-hall, thinking during the music of Hume's science of human nature or Kant's categorical imperative. He had great sympathy with Kant's ethical views, though he deplored that great philosopher's misunderstanding of Judaism. He had already planned, and was later to write, an essay on Kant and Judaism in which he showed that Kant's ethical theories were really compatible with the traditional Jewish view if only he had understood it.

The family extricated itself from the cabs and, ushered in by the President of the Edinburgh Hebrew Congregation, entered the door of 18 Lonsdale Terrace and climbed to the first floor, to the unexpectedly capacious flat that was to be their home for some months. Its large drawing-room overlooked the Meadows, which the rabbi now looked down on with a feeling almost of triumph. He remembered the stuffy little room where as a small boy by the light of rush candles stuck in the wall he had carefully gone over the complicated legal arguments of a passage from *Baba Mezia*, 'the Middle Gate', a tractate of the Talmud that began with a discussion of the laws governing found property. He had always found legal discussions fascinating, and preferred them to those portions of the Talmud dealing with ritual. He also liked the agricultural passages in the tractate *Zeraim*, 'seeds', and often thought of the paradox that Judaism, originally an agricultural religion with its festivals geared to the farmer's year, had for centuries been studied in walled-in ghettos by sedentary scholars who had never had the opportunity even to see a farm. And now there was the Meadows, not a farm, but a fine green open space, symbol of the new liberated world into which he was to bring his Jewish traditions and his Jewish faith.

He was entering the broad uplands of civilisation. Scotland, he remarked to his wife, was the one country in Europe that had never persecuted the Jews, though he added with wry honesty that that was in some degree because Jews arrived there late and in small numbers. But there was also the Presbyterian factor, the traditional Scottish exaltation of the Old Testament and regard for the Jews as the People of the Book. What a synthesis: Judaism, Hume, Kant and the Scottish Calvinist tradition.

The German synthesis had broken down. By the time of the outbreak of the First World War he was a well established British citizen with an English-born Jewish wife and three English-born children. The Germany of Goethe and Schiller and Kant and Beethoven — a Germany he had loved—had disappeared from view in the Kaiser's Germany and, as he told his Sunderland congregation, they ought to be proud and happy to be living in a free and enlightened democracy where tolerance was guaranteed and personal liberty a tradition. It was right to fight for these things against forces that opposed them. He read less and less German and more and more English. And now he had a wife and children who were native English speakers. And his children were now going to be educated in Edinburgh, a proud prospect.

Standing in this northern capital, he could define his position with respect both to his past and his future. He looked back across the years of *golus* to ancient Israel, where, ever since the Balfour Declaration of two years before, he saw the emergence of a revived Jewish state which would provide cultural and spiritual regeneration for all the Jewish people. This did not mean that he would ever contemplate emigration to Palestine. There would always be a Jewish diaspora, always be a fruitful interaction between Jewish and secular western culture, and currents would flow from a new Jewish state to produce an even richer interpretation of Jewish tradition as well as of civilisation as a whole. He had a role to play there! He would engage with the world of contemporary Scottish literati and he would also form in Edinburgh a centre of Zionist activity that would support the formation of a Jewish state and help to educate the gentiles in an understanding of its universal function. To the new state could and should go the oppressed and under-privileged Jews of Eastern Europe to develop their traditions in freedom. He enjoyed that freedom already.

But what about those student years in Germany? Arguments in Bierstuben about Kant's categorical imperatives, discussions about Hume's view of history, reading of German poetry, listening to German music, moving in a milieu of sophisticated western culture? Well, what about all that? Had he never felt that the world of strict dietary laws, rigorous daily Hebrew praying, meticulous observance of the sabbath and festivals, and the whole tradition of talmudic interpretation of what at bottom was a fundamentalist reading of the Pentateuch — *Torah mi-shamayim*, the Law from Heaven — was in some way incompatible with that free intellectual and cultural life? Did God *really* dictate the Law to Moses? On this basis all Jewish religion rested. What did he actually believe about all this — he, an orthodox rabbi with unimpeachable rabbinical qualifications as well as a German doctorate in philosophy? Had there been moments of doubt in his student years? Could he really reconcile studying the Talmud by rush candles in a Yiddish-speaking *shtetl* with the free intellectual and cultural life of an educated Westerner? Well, there was Moses Mendelssohn. There were Kant's views on ethics that could be interpreted Mosaically. There was undoubtedly the fact that if people did not believe that the moral law had divine sanction, they could not be counted on to obey it. And there was pride in his Jewish background and ancestry. He *had* worked it out. Here, looking out on the Meadows from the window of the drawing-room in Lonsdale Terrace, he was confident that he had worked it out.

He had accepted the yoke. 'The yoke of the law' was the traditional Jewish phrase. He was a rabbi, he had accepted it, his duty was to expound it, interpret it. And defend it. He knew how to defend it; he had the western philosophical tools. He would show that one did not have to be simple-minded, superstitious, credulous, to be able to accept the rigours of Jewish orthodoxy. Do not eat milk with meat, do not light a fire on the sabbath, do not eat anything that had even been anywhere *near* anything leaven on Passover. There was a wisdom here, a rationality, a humanist explanation. Ah, but that was not why Jews were commanded to do these things. It was because God ordered it, in his inscrutable wisdom. And the rabbis of the Talmud interpreted the word of God through their own dialectical system, not through liberal humanist justification.

Moses had told the Children of Israel that it was for them to choose: they could choose to obey the Law of God, which meant life, or they could choose to disobey it, which meant death. That was a good line, that was the rabbi's line: a society lived by the law, by proper ethical behaviour, otherwise it would destroy itself. Proper ethical behaviour might not necessarily produce happiness or prosperity for an individual, but it produced health in the community. The Mosaic law was about the community, was it not? But surely it was about individual behaviour? Categorical imperatives again. There could be no good life without them.

It was a weary business, sometimes, trying to fit Jewish orthodoxy into a scheme of rational humane ethics. Yet it was *his* business, his destiny indeed. He would, he knew, walk to the Graham Street synagogue every Saturday morning from the flat in Lonsdale Terrace as he would do later from his own house on the other side of the Meadows, and preach a Judaism that was both traditional and rational. Thought was free: *Die Gedanken sind frei*, in the words of one of the songs he had sung as a student in Berlin. It was behaviour that mattered. Rabbinical Judaism, as he was fond of pointing out, did not preach an ortho*doxy* but an ortho*praxis*: it was not what you thought but what you did that mattered. Then why all this fuss about philosophy? Why write about Kant and Judaism? What it amounted to was this: you had to know your own position, intellectually as well as morally. He muttered in Greek Archimedes' famous statement: 'Give me a place to stand and I shall move the world.' He had a *pou stō*, a place to stand: *Torah im derech eretz* here in Presbyterian Edinburgh.

He had stood elsewhere. He had stood *shokling* with religious fervour facing the ark, reciting the eighteen benedictions, in a stuffy *shul* in Neustadt–Scherwindt. And he had sat at home hour after hour over an enormous *shas*, (Talmud volume), construing from Aramaic into Yiddish the convoluted arguments of long-dead rabbis. He had walked, too, along cobbled streets where Jewish stall-holders sold everything from pickled herring to sabbath candles. He had walked sedately home with his father and brother from *shul* through Jewish lanes to a sabbath meal of soup and chicken, with a brief Hebrew grace recited beforehand and a very long one sung afterwards. (Very Jewish, he once remarked cheekily to his father as a boy, not to give proper thanks for food until you have made sure that you have had it.) And he had walked in the Tiergarten in Berlin and in the streets of Leipzig, discussing, arguing, relishing the thrust of argument with fellow students. No one trained in talmudic dialectics needed to be taught how to argue.

The drawing-room in Lonsdale Terrace smelt of furniture polish. Someone had been smartening the place for his family's arrival. Furniture polish was not a particularly Jewish smell. His father's house in Leeds, now: that had a very Jewish smell, Jewish cooking mingled with cigar smoke. He recalled the smells of Vilna and of Neustadt: street smells, house smells, the musty smell of the *sefer torah* as he kissed it when it was being carried round the synagogue, the smell of the spice-box sniffed in turn by each member of the family at the end of the sabbath, to comfort one for the departure of that blessed day of rest. There was the inky smell of schoolrooms, the wooden smell of university lecture theatres, the theatre smell of sweat and perfume. Ah yes, he had seen *Die Lustige Witwe* in Berlin, wearing his dress-coat and white tie, and he had seen the ladies in their décolleté dresses. That was a seductive world. The same young man who had eaten his kosher dinner in the back room of a butcher's shop was all dressed up in a theatre, a *goyischke* theatre, a *goyischke* atmosphere. How his life had been made up of contrasts! Rashi and David Hume, *Die Lustige Witwe* and *L'cho dodi*, 'Come, my beloved', the song to the Princess Sabbath sung at the Friday evening service. He had composed a song for his elder brother's wedding in Hamburg. His brother had married a Hamburg Jewish girl, and the song he had composed for the wedding was in German, except for the Latin tag at the end of each verse. It was about the change of state for bride and groom and it had the refrain:

O jingle jangle jerum,
O quae mutatio rerum.

Mutatio rerum, indeed.

The rabbi liked Latin tags. *Mens sana in corpore sano* he would quote to his young sons, encouraging them to take healthy walks (but not to indulge in sports: he was wholly indifferent to organised sport). And when the boys had to wash their hands ritually before each meal, reciting a Hebrew blessing during the operation, their father would mutter *alter alterum lavat*, 'one [hand] washes the other' (but his son speculated many years later that as *manus* was feminine shouldn't it have been *altera alteram lavat*?) If people did not believe in a divine law and acted in accordance with their individual desires and beliefs, the rabbi would say that the world would be plunged into a perpetual *bellum omnium contra omnes*. And when he expressed himself on a controversial question he was careful to be *fortiter in re, suaviter in modo*. Now that he was in Scotland, he reflected, he must quote Burns. 'A man's a man for a' that.' 'To see ourselfs as others see us.' He knew his Burns.

But of course Hebrew tags were his professional baggage. He had one, from Bible or Talmud, for almost every situation. The Jewish religion also had a blessing for almost every occasion. The one to be recited at having arrived at a special point in one's life, a *she-hechayanu*, thanked God for having preserved and sustained one to reach this experience. Looking out at the Meadows, the rabbi recited it now under his breath. The blessing ended with the phrase *ad ha-yom hazeh*, 'up to this day'. The rabbi's sermons were full of anticipations of a great day, a great day of emancipation, a great day of the return to their ancient land of the people of Israel, a great day when once again the Law should go forth from Zion, the great day promised at the end of the central Jewish prayer *alenu*, 'when the Lord shall be one and his name one'.

And this grey February day in Edinburgh? A great day

for him indeed, but how was it related to the hopes and yearnings of the Jewish people that he had often so eloquently expressed? Would the Messiah come in Scotland? The rabbi did not believe in a literal personal Messiah; he believed in historical movements, in progress, in amelioration, and in the acceleration of movement in the right direction by the actions of individuals. A flourishing Jewish community in Scotland respected by the Scots and interacting fruitfully with them without either party giving up its own traditions and religious practices — that would, metaphorically, speed the coming of the Messiah, of the great day, and he could help there. And if an elderly woman came to see him with the innards of a chicken wrapped in newspaper to ask a *sh'eilah*, a question of Jewish law concerning whether that particular chicken — having perhaps swallowed a pin or in some other way rendered its *kashrut* dubious — was edible, he gave his verdict according to talmudic law, what had this to do with progress, with the coming of the great day? His father had been known for his leniency in interpreting talmudic law; he had engaged in a notable controversy concerning the *mikvah* or ritual bath and had been accused by the ultra orthodox of deviation into laxity, yet he was still a Jewish rabbi and scholar isolated from his English environment in his Yiddish-speaking congregation. He was pleased that his son had been appointed rabbi in Edinburgh, but not for the reasons that gave his son such pleasure. This was one of the many ways of perpetuating the Jewish tradition in the *golus*: it was not a step in some great march of progress.

But for the younger rabbi it was a great beginning. Let the old ladies ask their *sh'eilahs*: he would attend to them faithfully enough: others would dream dreams and see visions and an enlightened world would see a living Judaism as a great moral force in civilisation. For was he not living in a great free country in a great free age? And could not now *Torah im derech eretz* be given a vibrant new meaning in the city of David Hume and the Scottish literati? *Fiat justitia ruat coelum*, he once wrote, was a stupid slogan, for the sole purpose of *justitia* was to serve human welfare, as the rabbi and Hume agreed. Yet he disagreed with Hume on the source of *justitia*, which was divine. He noted with pleasure that the motto of his newly adopted city came from the Psalms: *nisi dominus frustra*: 'except the Lord build the city, they labour in vain that build it'. The Hebrew word for 'builders' and the Hebrew word for 'children' are almost identical, and there is a notable rabbinical gloss that virtually equates the two. He would found a Jewish–Scottish dynasty, and there would be children to build. His children were in fact at this moment exploring the Meadows.

Quantum mutatus ab illo: the rabbi thought of the Virgilian phrase as he stood looking at the green expanse out of the window. From the cobbled streets of an East European ghetto to the elegance of the Athens of the North. And perhaps also the Jerusalem of the North? On previous visits to Edinburgh he had noticed public buildings modelled on classical temples, which were however rather different from Solomon's temple or the second temple that replaced it or even Herod's re-building. Yet buildings were a link between cultures and religions. The rabbi had joined the Freemasons, partly because the order welcomed all believers in God and did not profess a christological theology, and partly because he was fascinated by the masonic imagery taken from the stories and legends of the Jerusalem Temple. Here was the Hebrew Bible put to a remarkable new use. Intrigued as he was by the Freemasons' use of the Temple, and praying as he did daily (as did all orthodox Jews) for the restoration of that ancient House of God, the rabbi had yet no great passion for the priestly tradition. It was the ethical law and the eloquent preaching of the Prophets that provided his foundations, and the rabbinical rather than the priestly tradition that most appealed to him. He did not believe that all modern Jews who bore the surname Cohen were literally *cohanim*, descendants of Aaron the first priest, and so entitled to the special priestly privileges laid down in the Pentateuch. The priestly benediction recited on High Festivals, when all the Cohens assembled to bless the congregation in the old biblical words of benediction, had been abolished by the rabbi in his Sunderland synagogue and he would not allow it in Edinburgh either. No tailor or watchmaker would assert religious authority over *him*, even if his name was Cohen. He, the rabbi, was the spiritual leader of his people, and he would bless them from the pulpit, as he blessed each *barmitzvah* boy at the end of the little homily he would give him after the sermon. 'May the Lord bless you and keep you . . . May the Lord turn his face towards you and grant you peace.'

Yes, peace. *Shalom*. The Great War had been the war to end war. And pogroms were steadily receding into history. Peace and Progress. Enlightenment. Some day — perhaps, even, *beyamenu*, in our time — a new Temple would be built in Jerusalem, the word of God would go forth again out of Zion to enrich the culture of the West, and here in the Jerusalem of the North he would proclaim a revived Jewish message to Jew and Gentile. This would give a new meaning to *Torah im derech eretz*. The old rabbis of Vilna and all those others behind them, the *gaonim* and *roshei yeshivah*, the tosefists and talmudists and commmentators back to Rashi, back to Judah Ha-Nasi and back further to the Hebrew prophets and to the original lawgiver, *Moshe rabbenu*, Moses our teacher, they would all be given a new meaning, the old message delivered with a new richness. *Chadesh yamenu ke-kedem* they chanted in the synagogue as the scroll of the Torah was returned to the ark: 'renew our days as of old'. Yes, there would be renewal as well as return. Two thousand years of guardianship of tradition in bitter exile would be justified at last. The Messiah was not a person, but a historical ideal. God, the rabbi was in the habit of telling his congregation, works in history. There is a divine plan. But it needed men of vision to implement it. Here in this northern capital he would play his part.

Meanwhile, in the *beth hamedrash*, the house of study, attached to the synagogue on Richmond Street, the *shul* of the immigrant Yiddish-speaking Edinburgh Jews, old men were hunched over a volume of the Talmud studying the problems that arose if a man who lived in the Land of Israel near the border had a fruit-tree in his garden one of whose branches leaned over into a foreign country. If some fruit fell from the tree on to the foreign side, were tithes still payable on it? The Aramaic text was translated into Yiddish by the leader of the group, and in the sing-song voice that had become characteristic of talmudic argument, pros and cons were argued in the latter language. The rabbi was now the spiritual leader of these men too — he had been 'called' to Edinburgh by both congregations, the English-speaking one that worshipped in Graham Street and the 'greener *shul*' on Richmond Street — which he was determined to unite. If Richmond Street represented *Torah* and the city of Edinburgh *derech eretz*, what was the synthesis? Not, surely, the Scots Yiddish spoken by some of the elderly immigrants from Lithuania, which was an ephemeral cultural oddity. In his mind the rabbi was planning a book of essays in which he would explain what the true synthesis should be, how Hume and Kant could be related to the Torah, how talmudic argument and what he called in the Hebrew sermon he contributed to a book of his father's *ha-philosophim*, the philosophers of the Enlightenment, could be brought into a symbiosis. *Yehi or*, 'let there be light', God had said at the beginning of the Creation. Now let there be Enlightenment, *Aufklärung*. He had studied Talmud by candlelight as a boy; his house in Sunderland was lit by gas; here in Edinburgh he enjoyed electric light that could be switched on and off with a flick of the fingers. As the February dusk deepened he switched on the electric light in the Lonsdale Terrace drawing-room. '*Yehi or*,' he said, 'let there be light'; '*va-yahi or*', 'and there was light'. Outside, the lamplighter with his pole was on his rounds, lighting up the street gas-lights one by one. The rabbi's wife had bought for the children a copy of Stevenson's *A Child's Garden of Verses* as in a way an introduction to Edinburgh. The rabbi had dipped into it, and had been especially struck by the poem about the lamplighter. He had learned that Stevenson had come from a family of lighthouse engineers. A good metaphor, he thought, for the work he had set himself: lighthouse engineering. It was dark outside now, but the street lights shone brightly.

II

Waverley Station again, in the early spring of 1925. A photographer from *The Scotsman* was focusing on the rabbi as he stood on the platform, flanked by senior members of his congregation, before boarding a train to London en route to Palestine to participate in the opening of the Hebrew University in Jerusalem. It was an occasion, and he savoured it. He was now the most prominent Jewish character in Scotland, spokesman for his people and its culture to all Scots, and in a sense a Scot himself, for he identified himself closely with the Scottish people and saw the Jews in Scotland as a cultural minority forming part of a many-patterned society. Were there not still Gaelic-speaking communities in the Highlands? An eccentric Free Kirk minister in Lewis kept writing him letters in which he proved to his own satisfaction that Gaelic was based on Hebrew and the Gaels were the Lost Ten Tribes. The rabbi treated this fantasy with indulgent good humour: it was nonsense of course, but a pleasing nonsense which somehow authenticated the Jewish role in Scotland. More significant was his friendship with the Professor of Hebrew at Edinburgh University (a Church of Scotland minister) with whom he had many stimulating conversations. The Professor showed him an old Hebrew Bible in the Advocates' Library and, pointing to what appeared to be faded blood-stains, said grimly that they were probably a memorial to some old Jewish massacre somewhere in Europe. Telling this story at home, the rabbi observed (but to his family only) that the blood probably resulted from a recalcitrant pupil's nose-bleed when the *rebbe*, teaching children Hebrew in the *cheder* (Hebrew school), gave him a slap for inattention. Such slaps —

known as a *patz-af-ponim* in Yiddish — were not unknown
in the course of teaching children Hebrew: the old-fashioned
rebbe had the reputation of being short-tempered. For all
his romantic optimism, the rabbi was a realist in matters
of this kind.

But what about the Hebrew University to which he was
now bound? One of the very few wealthy members of his
congregation had offered to pay his fare to Palestine — the
rabbi's modest salary would not allow him to fund such a
journey himself — and he gratefully accepted. He had been
formally invited to attend the ceremony, and rejoiced that
he was enabled to accept the invitation. The party assembled
on the platform at Waverley symbolised the synthesis he
had achieved in Edinburgh, but where did he now stand
with respect to a Jewish National Home in Palestine and a
Hebrew University in Jerusalem? His position was crystal
clear: such a national home and such a national cultural
institution were to be the beacon with respect to which
Jewish life and thought could be illuminated and — equally
important — would be seen clearly and brightly performing
that function throughout the world. Roman Catholics did
not believe that they should all live in Rome, and Jews,
the rabbi maintained, should not consider it the duty of
all of them to migrate to Palestine. A small Jewish state
with a university of its own destined to international
greatness would guarantee the status of the Jewish people
throughout the world, and would perhaps in time purify
the Jewish religion from its superstitious ghetto accretions
and once again the Law would go forth out of Zion and the
Word of the Lord from Jerusalem. In Edinburgh he would
be oriented towards both Jerusalem and Scotland. Now it
was the Jerusalem side of the equation that beckoned more
seductively. Five years before he had stood in the same
railway station determined to carry rabbinic Judaism into
the Scottish Enlightenment and found a Scottish–Jewish
way of life that would contribute both to Scotland and to
Judaism. Now he was about to move temporarily in the other
direction, back to the well-springs of his own culture. And it

was to a Hebrew *university* he was going, the university being a western institution, an international symbol of learning and intellectual exploration. What an achievement, the founding of a university in Israel's ancient capital! He would come back to Edinburgh in due course, refreshed and inspired, to continue his synthesising mission.

And indeed he did come back refreshed and inspired, lecturing on his experience throughout the country, talking of the thrill of hearing the ceremony conducted throughout in the Hebrew language, boasting of having himself made a long speech in Hebrew without a note. In this way Judaism was to be purified of the *golus* (he still mentally pronounced this Hebrew word for exile in the Ashkenazi pronunciation in which he had been brought up rather than in the Sephardi way, *galut*, adopted by the modern Hebrew movement), and Jews in Scotland as in other western countries could consider themselves as privileged members of a multi-cultural society. In a sense his experience in Palestine in 1925 — the only occasion on which he went there — was a kind of exorcism of the ghetto memories of his childhood, the babble of Yiddish voices, the smells, the cobbled streets, the shawls of the women and the gaberdines of the men, the mixing of high religious experience and crude superstition. There, in the (literally) new Jerusalem, was to be the other pole in his work of reconciliation, the *torah* that went with *derech eretz*, not in a *shtetl* where men walked with shuffling gait and bowed shoulders.

The ghetto was gone, and good riddance. (It was not of course really gone: its elimination was to come about in the Second World War in a way that challenged every hope on which he had built his life.) Jerusalem and Athens, in the old phrase (but it was the Athens of the North now), could now relate to each other in a new symbiosis, uncluttered by that embarrassing middle term. And the modern Jewish student, always for the rabbi the symbol of Jewish regeneration, would not have to scrounge for the crumbs of western culture as Salomon Maimon had done so brilliantly and so tragically in the eighteenth century.

One of the rabbi's earliest essays had been on Salomon Maimon. He published it later in a volume called *Aspects of Judaism*, adding a paragraph expressing the hope — indeed the conviction — that no longer would Jewish students be subjected to the kind of ordeal that had destroyed Maimon. This collection of essays, which included the long meditated work on Kant and Judaism, he sent to the Professor of Logic and Metaphysics at Edinburgh University, whom he knew to be a Kant scholar. One winter Friday evening, when the rabbi and his family were assembled round the dining-room fire after welcoming the sabbath, the maid appeared at the door to announce that 'Mr Smith' had come to see him. He was astonished that anybody should come to see him on a Friday night, sacred to the family in all Jewish homes, and brusquely told the maid to show Mr Smith into the study. There was no fire in the study that night, and the room was cold and unfriendly. When the rabbi, in not the best of tempers, entered the study, he found that Mr Smith was Professor Norman Kemp Smith, come to give thanks for the book he had received. The rabbi was at once mollified, and the two shook hands warmly before sitting down in the chilly room to commence a conversation which soon revealed that the professor and the rabbi had been students at the University of Leipzig at the same time and had studied Kant under Paulsen. They might even have sat side by side on the same bench. When the rabbi, after a long interval, finally rejoined his family at the fireside, he was beaming. It was not only ex-Polish Jews who had studied philosophy in Germany: young men from Edinburgh had done so too. It was a satisfying thought.

By the mid-1920s the rabbi had established his *modus vivendi* in Edinburgh. Preaching eloquently every Saturday morning in the synagogue, presiding over Jewish religious education in the *cheder* evening classes which, thanks to his intervention with the city authorities, now met in the spacious Sciennes School and no longer in the damp basement of the Graham Street synagogue, he also orated about Robert Burns at Burns Clubs and travelled around

Scotland lecturing to audiences of all kinds on such subjects as Jewish ethics and the modern world. Every year he gave the inaugural address to the Edinburgh Jewish Literary Society: his optimistic idealism shone forth in his moral eloquence. He would regularly contribute to the correspondence columns of *The Scotsman*, letters defending, explaining and illustrating the Jewish point of view on a great variety of topics. Jerusalem and the Athens of the North. But had he really eliminated that third factor, those years of Yiddish-speaking ghetto life that stretched for centuries immediately behind him? There were reminders of it even in Edinburgh. At the Graham Street synagogue he preached in English. But there was the other Edinburgh synagogue in Richmond Street, in the heart of the old immigrant Jewish quarter, of which he was also the rabbi, where the elderly Yiddish-speaking worshippers had never heard of David Hume and some of whom were suspicious of the rabbi's synthesis. Here he was expected to speak in Yiddish when he attended once every few weeks (for Graham Steet was his main base) and his Germanised version of the language fell strangely on the ears of his listeners. But he was their rabbi; they came to him with their questions (voiced in Yiddish) about problems in rabbinical law, and he answered them out of his talmudic scholarship. And when he visited his father in Leeds they communicated orally in Yiddish (though they wrote to each other always in Hebrew). A small minority of the Edinburgh Jewish community were suspicious of a rabbi, however impeccable his talmudic credentials, who had a doctorate from a western university. A doctor yet? Where is it written that a rabbi should hold a doctorate?

You could not turn your back on a thousand years of Jewish history. The rabbi was uneasily aware of this, but chose to make his own selection of Jewish history. Modern Hebrew poets, yes; he read Bialik and Tchernikowski to his children; the great Hebrew poets of the Jewish Golden Age in early mediaeval Spain were another oasis he recommended for cultural refreshment; and of course the Hebrew prophets, especially his favourite Isaiah, of

whose book he had his children memorise whole chapters.
When he went through the Pentateuch with his children,
teaching them to translate from Hebrew into English each
word of each verse, he skipped those parts that dealt with
priestly laws and cultic ordinances and concentrated on
the narrative and on the ethical parts. Yet was not all of
the Pentateuch the Word of God, as narrated by him to
Moses? Again and again, in his preaching and his writing,
the rabbi argued that unless one insisted on the divine origin
of ethical commandments, people would feel free to ignore
them when they felt it was in their interest to do so. He
attacked 'Liberal' Judaism for its arrogant assumption that
we know what biblical precepts are acceptable and what are
not. Yet by sliding over so much of the Bible in the education
of his own children was he not implicitly making that very
assumption? But he slid over more than that. The whole
chassidic tradition was distasteful to him: Yiddish folk-song
and folklore never found their way into his household, and
he was embarrassed when anybody introduced them at
Jewish social gatherings. The Yiddish-speaking immigrant
Jewish traders and their lingua franca of Scots–Yiddish with
which they communicated with their gentile customers
were not often invited to the rabbi's house socially, as
were the English-speaking western-educated members of
the Graham Street synagogue. His children did not go to
their children's parties, but they went to the parties of what
might be called the Jewish upper-class families of Edinburgh.
To some of the Yiddish speakers this appeared as a kind
of snobbery. But the social implications were incidental: it
was really the rabbi's way of implementing *Torah im derech
eretz*, rabbinical Judaism and western culture.

The synthesis implied a sacrifice, though the rabbi never
saw it quite in those terms. He never wavered in his loyalty
to rabbinical Judaism, even if (like his father but more so) he
was generous in his interpretation of rabbinical law. When he
attended a Burns supper to propose the immortal memory
of the bard, there was always a special kosher haggis for the
rabbi, prepared and sent in by the Jewish butcher, but he

did not go so far as to insist on bringing his own knife and
fork. He would not countenance riding on the sabbath and
withdrew his children from school on every Jewish festival
that fell within the school term. He even intervened with
the university authorities to prevent examinations being
set on a Saturday or a Jewish festival.

The ghetto was a nightmare from which the Jews, the rabbi
believed, were now awakening. Yet was it not the ghetto that
had preserved the identity of the Jewish people throughout
all those Christian centuries? He knew his Jewish history; he
knew how tolerance and equality and open access by Jews to
all non-Jewish institutions could result in assimilation. And
that was always his dread. You could not have a synthesis
unless there were distinct elements to synthesise. These
thoughts sometimes troubled him. In the bad old days,
he told young members of his congregation at a special
children's service, a Jew could be called upon to die for his
people. No more: now a Jew was called upon to *live* for his
people. And how? By maintaining Jewish religion, Jewish
culture, and a knowledge of Jewish history while living fully
and freely in a largely non-Jewish environment. Surely with
the New Jerusalem now standing as a beacon this should
be a goal easily realised? Yet he knew there were strains,
and he knew what had happened to so many children
of the German–Jewish Enlightenment. It was indeed in
direct response to that knowledge that the Hildesheimer
ideal had been worked out. This was surely how God
worked in history, allowing a problem then throwing in
a solution. This was the same God whom he addressed
so fervently on that most solemn day of the Jewish year,
Yom Kippur. Clad in his white *kittel* he would intone the
traditional prayers and sing out instructions to the cantor
on the sounds to be blown on the *shofar*. He would preach
his eloquent evening sermon before the sun set and the
great fast came to an end. 'Open to us the gate, at the
time of the closing of the gate, for the day is fading,' he
would quote from the sonorous Hebrew prayer in a rapt
appeal to his audience to consider their relation to God

as Jews who were now shedding the communal guilt of another year of Jewish history. He was a different man on *Yom Kippur*. No thought of David Hume crossed his mind as he prostrated himself (on the one occasion in the year when it was proper to do so) while reciting the second paragraph of the great *alenu* prayer.

So: one could imagine an ironical voice from his childhood saying in Yiddish 'vos is dos fur a "synthesis"?' — what sort of a synthesis is this? Moods shifted. The personality itself could take on different colouring. Nevertheless the rabbi walked sedately through the streets of Edinburgh, saluted by Jew and Christian, a weel kent character bearing with him the dignity of his people and gestures of Jewish–Scottish fellowship.

III

Waverley Station on 1 August 1930. The rabbi was assembling his family on the platform before they embarked on the train for Fife. They were going away for their summer holidays, as all respectable Edinburgh families did, and they were going to Crail, a picturesque fishing village in the East Neuk where they had for some time been regular August visitors. The luggage — masses of it — had already been stowed in the luggage van by a helpful porter to whom the rabbi had given a silver sixpence. The train — the Fife Coast Express — crossed the Forth Bridge and ran up the coast, stopping at all the little towns frequented by summer visitors — Aberdour, Burntisland, Kinghorn, Kirkcaldy (but this was no holiday resort: the smell of the linoleum assailed the family's noses), Leven, Lundin Links, Largo, St Monans, Pittenweem, Anstruther, and then Crail. These names were all familiar to the rabbi and his family, as familiar as the names of the twelve tribes of Israel. On earlier holidays in Fife they had brought with them a trunk-full of dishes on which to eat kosher meat sent out by post by the Edinburgh Jewish butcher. But this became too arduous, and the rabbi's wife, who had to spend so much of the holidays dealing with these matters, decided that for the month of August they should avoid all meat and eat only fish and vegetarian dishes, which required no special utensils. This greatly eased the burden of preparing for the annual holiday, and as the Fife fish was splendid and the rabbi's wife, like all Jewish housewives, did marvellous things with fish, the family were wholly content with the arrangement.

Things were changing. On earlier holidays the rabbi had worn his habitual black garb, less formal than the frock-coat he wore on sabbaths and festivals, but still somewhat sombre in appearance. Gradually, under pressure from his growing children, now in their teens, he relaxed sartorially. He acquired grey flannel trousers and a blue blazer with brass buttons, and wore a soft grey shirt with a flowing tie, instead of the stiff white shirt and black bow tie he habitually wore. And he wore sometimes a tweed cap and sometimes a soft grey 'split-pea' hat.

So now he stood with his family on the platform of Waverley Station in his grey flannel trousers and blue blazer under a light overcoat, into whose pocket was thrust a copy of *The Scotsman*. This was an Edinburgh bourgeois family doing the Edinburgh bourgeois thing.

In the luggage were of course prayer books and a Hebrew Bible, for even on holiday mornings prayers were said in Hebrew (by the males, each donning his *tefilin* or phylacteries) and each sabbath the appropriate portion of the Law was read in Hebrew. But you could read your Hebrew Bible sitting on a bench in the Castle Walk (the family's rented house was on the corner of the Castle Walk) overlooking the sea and even sing quietly to yourself some appropriate Hebrew hymn while below the waves lapped gently on the rocks. Here was a real exercise in adjustment. During the week the family bathed in the sea, sprawled on the beach, walked to Balcomie or along the St Andrews road to Kingsbarns, or even took bus excursions to nearby towns. Sometimes they took the bus

— and very occasionally walked — to St Andrews and had tea at the Tudor Café after sitting on the beach and going for a swim. The rabbi had been taught to swim by his wife: swimming had formed no part of his education at the Königsberg *Gymnasium* or the Hildesheimer Seminary or the Universities of Berlin and Leipzig. He had no scruples now about consuming tea and scones in a Scottish café, though his father would never have dreamt of eating in a non-Jewish restaurant. Scrupulousness about meat was one thing: scones and buns and cakes were another, and he took care not to inquire too curiously into precisely what shortening ingredients had gone to their making. Yet Hebrew prayers chanted quietly on the Castle Walk testified to the fact that both elements of the Scottish–Jewish synthesis were still very much present.

He was still very much the rabbi, recognised as such by other visitors even in Crail. And the copy of *The Scotsman* that he had stuffed into his pocket before boarding the Fife Coast Express was not there simply to provide him with the news of the day: his alert eye would scan any item relevant to Jews or Judaism and sniff any suggestion of anti-semitism and, on holiday or not, he would write carefully reasoned letters to the editor whenever misinformation had to be corrected or prejudice censured. So, though he walked and swam and even ventured on golf in a peculiarly clumsy way, he always carried his people's honour with him. Indeed, he would reflect, it was coming more and more to this: he was the guardian of the honour and dignity of the Jewish people in Scotland. He would preach to his flock and remind them of Jewish principles and proper Jewish behaviour, but it was just as important — perhaps indeed more important? — that non-Jews should know what proper Jewish principles and behaviour were.

Sometimes, when walking with his family through rural Fife paths in late August, he would pluck an ear of wheat or barley or oats from a field they were passing, announce what it was, and meditatively chew a grain. He would then hold forth on the properties of each species. This surprised his children, who knew that their father had no agricultural experience and had led an exclusively urban life. 'It's all in the Talmud,' he explained with a smile. 'Judaism is all about agriculture; its festivals are all farmers' seasonal festivals. The Talmud is an agricultural manual, you know, as well as a lot of other things.' The rabbi glowed at being able to identify Fife grain from his background in that other world. He taught his children to recognise the different cereals in the field, while his wife quoted Tennyson on the reapers reaping early in among the bearded barley. Bearded barley, quite right, the rabbi said, holding up an ear.

The Jewish high festivals occurred very soon after the family's return home from their summer holiday, and the transition from the Fife holiday-maker to the rapt leader of a congregation celebrating the Creation and pleading for forgiveness of sins was a test of the rabbi's synthesis. He passed the test without difficulty: his weather-beaten holiday face radiated forth underneath his white biretta and above his white *kittel* like the countenance of Moses as he descended Mount Sinai with the tablets of the Law. He let the atmosphere carry him. Certain Hebrew chants and hymns that were part of the service for *Rosh Hashanah* and *Yom Kippur* moved him inexpressibly, as much for their associations as for their actual meaning. The plangent chanting of *Kol Nidrei* at the beginning of *Yom Kippur* did more to connect the rabbi with his past than any memories of childhood in the Ghetto. Here were the beauty and the mystery and the tradition that were beyond reason: the actual words of *Kol Nidrei* were bafflingly legalistic, but as the *chazan* chanted them in the synagogue the rabbi was moved with a deep sense of the wonder and beauty of Jewish liturgy.

So perhaps for all the luminous argument he presented in his essays and lectures, it was an irrational emotion, a mystical sense of tradition and continuity, that lay behind his Jewish loyalty and Jewish faith? Sitting on his favourite bench in the Castle Walk late in the evening as the sea grew dark and the sound of the splashing waves fell on his ears, he was aware of something in his response to experience that bore little relation to David Hume's philosophy and perhaps — perhaps — was something to do with the still small voice that spoke in the desert to his ancestors all those centuries ago. In Psalm 29, which was recited every sabbath just before the Torah scroll was returned to the ark, God is said to dwell in the flood. The sea that lapped the Fife coast was not perhaps very far from the sea of Jewish faith. Was he becoming a Nature mystic? He knew that this was a respectable English tradition, associated with Wordsworth, but this was something else, something that related the Firth of Forth to the *frisson* he got from listening to *Kol Nidrei*. This was not perhaps what the Hildesheimer teachers had meant by *Torah im derech eretz*, nor was it consonant with the view of that rabbi of the Talmud who held it to be sinful to break off the study of the Law to admire the beauties of Nature, but it was part of his experience, his synthesis. It was integral to the texture of his life. It would serve.

IV

Waverley Station again, twenty-one years after he had first arrived there with his family. Now he was meeting remnants of other Jewish families — refugee children who had managed to escape from Hitler's Germany and who were about to be looked after by Jewish communities in Scotland. The rabbi had watched the rise of Hitler's Germany with incredulous horror. He had refused to believe that when Hitler came to power he would implement the anti-semitic policy proclaimed in *Mein Kampf* (which the rabbi had read in German in an attempt to find out what the dangerous madman really believed). There was no talk yet of the 'final solution' but enough was now known about the position of the Jews in Germany to make it clear that the obsessive abuse of the Jews in *Mein Kampf* was being translated both into government policy which officially encouraged popular attacks. This was persecution, even more vicious than the mediaeval kind because it involved ousting from their positions in the professions and commerce patriotic German Jews who were fiercely loyal to the fatherland, many of whom had fought for Germany in the last war. The rabbi had been happy to side warmly with his adopted Britain against the Kaiser's Germany in that war: but this was a sort of Germany he had never dreamed of. His house in Edinburgh was open to German Jewish refugees and they came in dozens to enjoy hospitality and talk of their experiences. Some of them knew nothing of Judaism and had discovered their Jewish descent only when Nazi officials ferreted it out. This was no case of a religion that believed in its unique truth attacking infidels: it was something much more terrible, attacking people for their ancestry regardless of their beliefs or behaviour. Everything the rabbi had believed about the progressive amelioration of the Jewish lot was now challenged. And how could you have *Torah im derech eretz* if the *derech eretz* was so cruel and monstrous?

How could it all have happened, how was it possible? How could the enlightened modern world have allowed it? Talking with refugees in their native German — for some of them as yet had only rudimentary English — he repeatedly expressed his bewilderment and incredulity. 'Unglaublich ist es, unglaublich,' he kept repeating after a young German refugee doctor of no Jewish education or commitment described to him how Jewish doctors were being expelled from hospitals and forbidden to practise.

The rabbi clung to Britain as a rock of enlightenment and tolerance, and now that Britain was at war with Nazi Germany it was an absolute black-and-white situation, the war of right against might as he kept saying in his sermons. Yet this was a kind of conflict he had never anticipated: it arose from a situation that denied everything on which he had based his life and work. He was cheerful enough in greeting the children, patting them on the head or back, speaking words of comfort and hope, even joking occasionally. Yet it was a terrible business. These children might never see their parents again. And what were they guilty of? What were they to make of what had happened to them? What could he himself make of it? What for that matter did God make of it? Had not the Jews suffered enough over two thousand years? Was this a further punishment? He could not believe that. He could not agree with those orthodox rabbis who saw the Nazi attack on the Jews as punishment for their desertion of their religious traditions or (an even worse proposition) as a divine means of sending assimilated Jews back to their ancestral faith. The prophet Isaiah, whom he was so fond of quoting, had said that the people of Israel had already suffered double for all their sins, and there had been thousands of years of suffering since Isaiah. 'And because of our sins we were exiled from our land,' he recited with his congregation on *Rosh Hashanah*. Was God still punishing them, then? No: God was not involved in this. If he permitted it for his own mysterious reasons this did not mean that he willed it or wanted it. Man had free will and was responsible. But could Nazis be considered men? Could such cruel depravity be regarded as human? Was there a real active Devil after all, not merely an 'evil inclination', *yetser ha-rah*, that they prayed to have removed from them?

The only thing to do was to carry on teaching and preaching and comforting. He would extend a hand to all forces working against Hitler — as he was to do to the Soviet Union after it entered the war on the allies' side, in spite of his deep aversion to atheistic communism — and meanwhile expounded more eloquently than ever the main principles of Jewish tradition as he understood them, keeping to basic themes, the ethical foundations, the historical pattern, the meaning of the festivals in terms of Jewish imagination and Jewish hope. He knew with absolute certainty, even in the dark days of 1940 and 1941, that the allies would win the war. Hope was the word: *hatikvah*, the hope, was the title of the modern Jewish anthem. The rabbi would not give up hope. In spite of the shattering of his world, in spite of the *unglaublich*, the unbelievable, he would not revise his expectations — only push them further forward into the future. Nor would he retreat into an isolationist Jewish orthodoxy and renounce the western culture that could produce a Hitler. He knew well enough those elements in earlier German — and not only German — thought that had been drawn on in fashioning the Nazi view of the world; he knew the philosophers and anthropologists and others whose books were relevant. But — this was another of his Latin tags — *corruptio optimi pessima*, the corruption of the best produces the worst.

The rabbi was never more active in addressing non-Jewish audiences on such subjects as Jewish ethics and the place of the Jew in the modern world than he was in these war years. He would not forgo his synthesis. At the same time his Judaism became something more simple and moving — more prophetic and less rabbinic, perhaps — as he spoke and wrote of Jewish traditions and practices and their human appeal. The last work he produced was a series of essays for children on the meaning of the Jewish festivals. Amidst meetings and lectures and journeys in cold unlit trains (for his meetings and lectures took him far afield) as well as his weekly sabbath services and sermons, his long discussions with refugees, his polemical letters to newspapers when anything detrimental to the prestige of the Jews appeared, his talks with Jewish soldiers on leave, he steadily wore out his strength, refusing to give up any of his activities, concealing his growing illness, refusing to surrender to the collapse of the world of his younger optimistic hopes. As his health failed he strove to work even harder, for the tide of war was turning now and it was clear to all that Hitler was going to lose. By the end of 1944, ill and exhausted but pushing himself as hard as ever, he had moved to a position possibly unique among rabbis who considered themselves orthodox. An early and ardent Zionist, he was now increasingly opposed to the policies of Zionist activists and turned his attention more and more to the future position of the Jews in the diaspora. It sometimes seems that he almost despaired of his own generation and turned towards the young people: certainly children figured ever more largely in his thoughts and his activities. Those from Germany who had survived, those at home who had spent their childhood in the war years, they would build new bridges, create new hope, find a fruitful synthesis again. The biblical text he chose in one of his last sermons was the account of Jacob sending his beloved young son Joseph out to distant places to seek his brothers who were herding sheep. Some Jewish parents, he said, would blame Jacob for sending his darling son out to unknown dangers. But Jacob was right. He was right to send his son out to explore new experiences, for the old and traditional can only survive when they are continuously enriched by the new. It was as though the rabbi was forcing himself to see a new generation re-creating and fulfilling his dream.

He would not give up. It was not as though he were wrong: *they* were wrong. The great day would still come, the dream was still there. Victory was in sight. He knew he was dying now, lying in bed in the Edinburgh Royal Infirmary after an operation that came too late. Five more years, he said to his wife — his grown-up children were all away on war service — if only I had five more years: there is so much to do. The day before he died they told him Hitler was dead, and he smiled and murmured something about right over might. His wife was the only one by his bedside when he lapsed into unconsciousness and was soon afterwards pronounced dead by the doctor. It was some seconds after that, his widow later recorded, that she noticed a heaving in his chest and heard faintly the Hebrew words a Jew is supposed to recite at the moment of death, *Adonai hu ho-elohim*, the Lord is God. There, on 2 May 1945, in the Athens of the North, this talmudic student of David Hume and Immanuel Kant, this believer in *Torah im derech eretz*, this humane and liberal-minded prophet of accommodation and cultural pluralism, died in the tradition of his fathers with the old Hebrew affirmation of God on his lips.

Vilna, Neustadt, Königsberg, Berlin, Leipzig — all these

memories had been appropriated by Hitler. Edinburgh remained. Yet it was the words first learned as a small boy in an East European ghetto that heaved out from the chest of a man already pronounced dead. *Torah im derech eretz*: but in the end, in the extreme end, it was the Torah that stood alone.

It was a bright but cold day in early November 1991 on a sloping cul-de-sac of new houses, mostly still under construction, going off at right-angles from a street in north-east Edinburgh. Behind lay the main railway line from Edinburgh to the south: beyond the foot of the new street lay the old Roman road. The protective height of Arthur's Seat dominated the landscape to the south. There were flags flying. A showhouse, manned by men and women from the building firm responsible for the development, stood open and welcoming at the corner. A group of about fifteen people were assembled outside.

Lying propped against a low wall was a street-sign reading DAICHES BRAES. The new street was to be named after Rabbi Dr Salis Daiches, rabbi of the Edinburgh Jewish community from 1919 until his death in 1945, and this was the official naming ceremony. The late rabbi's two sons were asked to affix the new street sign while photographers clicked. Speeches were made. The rabbi's love of Edinburgh and his work for good community relations were referred to. Each of his sons gave a short account of the rabbi's involvement with the city. The cameras clicked again as the ceremony ended and the assembled company trooped into the showhouse for tea or coffee and a fine assortment of sandwiches (courtesy of the building firm).

One could almost see across to Piershill Cemetery where the rabbi had been buried forty-six years before. How he would have relished this occasion! It was an apotheosis he could never have imagined, a seal on his work for a Jewish community integrated in the city beyond anything he could have foreseen. This was the first street in Scotland to be called after a rabbi — probably the first street in Britain.

The idea came from one of the city councillors whose father had succeeded the rabbi as Grand Master of the Masonic Lodge Solomon and who was well aware of the rabbi's place in the religious and cultural life of the city. The rabbi had become a Freemason partly because this was an inter-faith organisation based on a belief in one God but with no overt reference to Christ in its ritual, partly because of its association with Solomon and his Temple, partly because it brought Jew and Gentile into social contact without compromising the beliefs and traditions of either. Lodge Solomon was not exactly a Jewish lodge; but its name had a Jewish ring to it and many Edinburgh Jews were members. Lodge Solomon was formally 'erected and consecrated' on 15 April 1920, just over a year after the rabbi arrived in Edinburgh and its first regular meeting, at which the rabbi was initiated, took place the following May. Now, after all these years, his masonic contacts had yielded this unexpected result.

So the rabbi's achievements rose up forty-six years after his death, all those years after his bitter disillusionment with the progress of civilisation caused by the rise of Nazism, to be commemorated in the name of a street in the city he had so enthusiastically adopted. What would they think, those Edinburgh citizens who would make their home there, of the significance of the name? The children riding their bicycles up and down the cul-de-sac would know that they lived in Daiches Braes. It would be just a name to them — an address. But for the rabbi it would have been, in the old biblical phrase, *yad va-shem*, 'a monument and a name', or rather a name as a monument, a name being the best kind of monument. *Yad va-shem* was the name given to the grimly moving museum of the Holocaust in Jerusalem, a very different kind of memorial. Here, in the capital of one of the few European countries which, as the rabbi had said at the opening of the new synagogue in 1932, had never shed Jewish blood, his memorial was an everyday street, a work-a-day street, a street which, though new now, would settle down as an indistinguishable part of suburban Edinburgh, not special, not different, sharing the ordinary rhythms of Edinburgh life.

To share in the ordinariness of the city: that was the greatest achievement. To be there, to be accepted, to be a more or less indistinguishable part of its urban life, the rabbi's street accepted like any other street, was a unique achievement. The rabbi's father, who had emigrated from an East European ghetto to spend the rest of his life in an exclusively Jewish quarter of Leeds and since 1937 had lain buried in the Jewish cemetery on a hillside on the outskirts of the city, would have been puzzled and amazed. This was the end of the road that had begun when he sent his children to a secular *Gymnasium* in Germany. A street was the end of the road. Was it symbolic that it was a cul-de-sac?

Who could tell? It seemed in May 1945 that here was the end of the story, and the rabbi's love affair with Edinburgh had ended with the affirmation of his ancestral creed at the moment of death. But a momentum of which he was unaware was gathering year after year until finally *Torah im derech eretz* became a rabbi's name commemorated in an Edinburgh street. The literal meaning of *derech eretz* is 'way of the land'. The name of that way turned out to be Daiches Braes.

'Braes' means 'slopes', and Daiches Braes was a sloping street. It is not known who decided to give a special Scots dimension to this street's name, but the rabbi would certainly have appreciated that. He used to be amused when eccentric ministers wrote to him trying to prove that Gaelic and Hebrew were related languages and that the original Scots were the Lost Ten Tribes. One correspondent went further and quite unhistorically (for the history of the name is known) proved to his own satisfaction that 'Daiches' was a Gaelic version of the Scots surname Home or Hume. The Gaelic for 'home' is 'dachaidh', which of course could easily have been corrupted to 'Daiches'. Once in the early 1920s the Daiches family spent their summer holidays on the Fife coast in a house called 'Mo Dhachaidh', 'My Home'. When the rabbi addressed the labels on his luggage the address began

Rabbi Dr Salis Daiches
'Mo Dhachaid'

The porter on reading the labels remarked that it was not necessary to have the name written twice.

Once was enough, especially if it was affixed permanently to an Edinburgh street. Jews in the popular imagination were often associated with rich bankers like Rothschild. The banks now associated with the rabbi were banks and braes, appropriately enough, for the rabbi knew and loved that Burns song. His volume of poems by the Hebrew poet Saul Tchernichowsky contained Hebrew renderings of some of Burns's poems, which he used to read to his children.

A street is where daily life is enacted, where, as Dr Johnson observed, a man on his way to a funeral may meet a man returning from a wedding. Life goes on: a Jew on returning from the funeral of one of his close relatives eats a ritual egg, symbol of germination, growth, the continuity of life. No seats are placed in Jewish cemeteries because (as the rabbi explained to his children) it is not good that one should sit in the cemetery and grieve for a lost loved one. There are prescribed rituals of mourning, and when they are over one must return to the world and carry on. Preserve memory, yes. *Zichrono livracha*, may his memory be for a blessing, one said in referring to a dead relative or indeed any dead person one had loved or respected, and to remember was a positive injunction in the Jewish creed. Judaism was indeed based on historical memory; it was a historical religion. At the same time it emphasised continuity, the dailiness of daily living, the centrality of the quotidian. And that takes us back to the street. The daily bustle of a street — people going out to work in the morning and returning in the evening, postmen arriving, children emerging to play (being a cul-de-sac, Daiches Braes had no through traffic), skipping, chanting, experimenting with tricycles and bicycles, folk meeting and standing to chat — that was to be the unconscious way in which the rabbi was to be commemorated in his adopted city.

The diversity of things in this world was noted in Jewish prayer and praise. Jews had a blessing for *everything*, every experience, every object. And when they were stumped for a particular blessing they had the all-purpose one: 'Blessed art thou O Lord who createst all manner of things.' There is a little four-line poem in the talmudic tractate entitled *Berachot*, 'Blessings', which in translation goes like this:

> Blessed be he who has left nothing at all out of his world,
> Who has created in it beautiful creatures
> And beautiful trees
> That men may look on them with delight.

And blessed be he who has created Daiches Braes where Edinburgh men, women and children can go about their business of work and play in the shadow of a Jewish rabbi's name.

What's in a name? Everything, according to Jewish tradition. According to Genesis, Adam gave names to all the creatures according to their natures. People's names were changed when their destiny changed: Abram became Abraham, Sarai became Sarah, Jacob became Israel. The Hebrew Bible is full of folk etymologies of both personal and place names: 'and so they called that place . . .'. The ineffable name of God was in a special category: the Psalmist praised his *name*, Moses and the prophets spoke in his *name*, and orthodox Jews referred to God simply as *ha-shem*, 'the Name'.

But the best thing, if you have a street named after you, is for the name to cease to be special as soon as possible, so that it becomes part of the landscape and taken for granted as such. That is the best kind of urban memorial, integrated into its environment.

And yet . . . integration was not a word the rabbi would ever have used. While he wanted the members of his congregation to be full and free citizens of Edinburgh, participating in all ways in the life of the city and contributing to its culture, he insisted on the importance of their maintaining their Jewish traditions and identity. Where would that leave Daiches Braes? Would not the resonance of the name Daiches be lost as the street became more and more accepted as just one more city street? Who could say? There was a tension here that corresponded to the one that lay at the heart of the rabbi's lifelong ambition to establish the Jewish community in Scotland as a full and recognised element in Scottish demography and Scottish culture. *Torah im derech eretz* again. It was a balancing act, a tight-rope walk. In a fully enlightened age, the rabbi always felt, it should not be so; it should be a natural form of what we today call cultural pluralism. Synthesis but not integration was his motto: the difference for him was very real. Perhaps Daiches Braes represented a synthesis, a symbol of an enlightenment not yet fully achieved in other areas. Blessed art thou O Lord who put into the minds of men the decision to call an Edinburgh street Daiches Braes.

'Her ways are ways of pleasantness and all her paths are peace.' The rabbi had chanted these words (in Hebrew) with his congregation every sabbath when they returned the scroll of the Torah to the ark. The ways referred to were the ways of the Torah, of divine law. Would Daiches Braes be a way of pleasantness? It would certainly soon become one of what Shelley called 'the trodden paths of men', but was there any guarantee that its association with a rabbinical name would lend it any special moral quality?

That would be asking too much, the rabbi himself would have said. Enough that it anchored his name permanently in Edinburgh, to become one of the city's sights and sounds. Those sights and sounds had from the first time he became aware of them been associated with freedom and enlightenment. They were anti-Ghetto sights and sounds, and his life had been a flight from the Ghetto. The clattering of the cable cars in the early 1920s, to be succeeded by the more swooshing sound of electric tram-cars;

the rattling carts with Leitch's lemonade and other mineral waters; the rumbling coal-carts with their attendants crying COAL, BRIQUETTES; the metallic noise of the milk cans delivered by boys in the early morning; the quick step of the lamplighter on winter afternoons as he bore his pole from lamp-post to lamp-post (ah, the lamplighter, that favourite symbolic figure); the tread of the uniformed postman delivering the morning mail; the soft thump of the *Scotsman* newspaper as it fell on the floor of the hallway having been pushed through the letter-box; the cries of the newsboy under Wellington's statue by Register House — 'SPATCH, NEWS; the speeding of bogies and guiders manipulated by small boys along pavements (the slope of Daiches Braes would make it ideal for such vehicles, but they had disappeared now); the puffing of unseen trains along Princes Street Gardens; the tuneless singing of beggars in the back greens of Livingstone Place; the summer music wafted from the grandstand in the Meadows; the skipping rhymes chanted by small girls as they demonstrated their skipping skills on the pavement; the barrel-organ with its melancholy tum-ti-tum churned out by its ragged owner; the pedalling knife-grinder sharpening the knives collected from the street's housewives; the tumultuous cries of assorted children released into the playground of Sciennes School; the chugging engine of the taxi waiting to take the rabbi and his family to Waverley Station for the beginning of their annual holiday — these were all Edinburgh sounds that as the 1920s moved into the 1930s became more and more familiar to the rabbi, more and more the sounds of *his* city, displacing all memories of the ghettos of Vilna and Neustadt. They would go on — different now, of course, as times changed, but still Edinburgh sounds — in Daiches Braes, the Edinburgh street that, although nobody would know it, represented the end of a journey that had begun in Vilna. Moses led the children of Israel out of Egypt to freedom, but never himself entered the Promised Land. And the rabbi never saw his Edinburgh street.

*   *   *

On the other side of Edinburgh there used to be an area of Morningside known as Little Egypt, and many streets in that district have biblical names. The Israelites escaped from Egypt to the land of Canaan, but in south Edinburgh Egypt and Canaan are intertwined in one another. Canaan Lane and Nile Grove are both in the former Little Egypt, as are Jordan Lane and Jordan Bank. There was once a farm in the area known as Egypt. It is said that the name of Canaan is mentioned in connection with this area as early as 1671 and that the Covenanters were responsible for these biblical associations. It is doubtful if any of the respectable inhabitants of Morningside — one of the most determinedly respectable of all districts of Edinburgh — ever reflects on the significance of the biblical element in their street names. They certainly do not consider themselves to have any Semitic or Egyptian associations.

People have a surprising lack of curiosity about the names of streets in which they live. And these names are redolent of history. Candlemaker Row in the Old Town really did house candlemakers (the hall of the Corporation of Candlemakers was built there in 1722); there was once a pottery in Potter Row; Earl Grey Street was named by a liberal Town Council after the popular champion of the Reform Bill; Eyre Place was named not after the notorious Governor of Jamaica who put down a slave revolt with great cruelty (and was defended by Thomas Carlyle) but after a brewer of that name who moved his Canongate brewery to the north side of Edinburgh in the early nineteenth century; Sciennes Road reminded the knowledgeable that the convent of St Catherine of Sienna was once situated there, though when the rabbi conducted evening Hebrew classes in Sciennes School it is doubtful if he knew of its saintly Christian association. Lonsdale Terrace, where the rabbi and his family stayed when they first came to Edinburgh, was called not after the Earls of Lonsdale (although other streets nearby such as Panmure Place and Brougham Street were called after noblemen) but after the nineteenth-century physician Henry Lonsdale who worked at the nearby Royal

Infirmary. Millerfield Place, where the rabbi spent most of his Edinburgh years, was unromantically called after a Mr Miller on whose property the street was built: he was the father of the engraver William Miller. Crawfurd Road, where the rabbi spent his last years, is adjacent to Minto Street, called after Lord Minto who, when Governor of Bengal, took with him an orientalist (who had also studied medicine) named Crawfurd after whom the former street was named when it was built in 1875. The powerful Dick and Lauder families, who intermarried, gave their names to Dick Place and Lauder Road while their relations are commemorated in other street names in the neighbourhood. More recent Edinburgh streets — those in the Inch housing scheme — are called after the titles of Scott's novels or characters in them — Redgauntlet Terrace, Ivanhoe Crescent, Ashton Grove (Lucy Ashton, the tragic heroine of *The Bride of Lammermoor*) and others. So Daiches Braes is in pretty mixed company.

Doubtless some future historian of the city will note that Daiches Braes was called after an Edinburgh rabbi. But will he understand what lay behind it? Will he realise that this was the end of a road? And will he appreciate how subtle, how problematical, how fraught with contradictions and paradoxes that road was? 'Make straight in the desert a highway for our God.' This sentence, from the fortieth chapter of Isaiah, the rabbi's favourite biblical book, is strange and haunting. What desert? How does God need a highway? Daiches Braes could hardly be called a highway for our God. Or perhaps it could? Perhaps cunning talmudic explicators would say: 'Yes, that is what we must understand by this phrase, an Edinburgh street called after a rabbi learned in Jewish law and lore. Would not that be a highway for our God?' Perhaps the little boy balancing precariously on a bicycle on Daiches Braes would bear that out. A highway for our God. A street where people fulfil themselves. The rabbi, who was a student of David Hume as well as the Talmud, would have accepted that. At least, it appears that he would. But we shall never know.

One hears, or used to hear, of street Arabs, homeless waifs who begged in the streets, but whoever heard of street Jews? Jews did not beg in the streets. They looked after their own, through the Jewish Board of Guardians. The Jews of Edinburgh in the rabbi's time were not rich. Many made a precarious living as travellers selling haberdashery out of battered suitcases to the wives of fishermen on the Fife coast. Many were small shopkeepers. Some were tailors, a few were watchmakers. A very few really prospered, one or two as successful proprietors of large furniture stores. Each group had its own relationship to the city. Most walked its pavements frequently, the older ones stooping slightly, often with hands behind back like the Duke of Edinburgh. It is forbidden to ride on any form of transport on sabbaths and festivals, so pious Jews got good practice in walking.

The rabbi could be seen regularly walking to the synagogue, in the 1920s across the Meadows and up Chalmers Street to the Graham Street *shul* (the building and even the street have now gone) and from the early 1930s up Minto Street to Salisbury Road and the new synagogue he had been instrumental in building. (Salisbury Road was not, as at least one newspaper-delivery boy believed, called after the rabbi's first name, Salis.) On weekdays he wore a soft black hat with a brim somewhat wider than that of a homburg; on sabbaths and festivals he wore a silk hat, that symbol of British respectability retained by Jews long after it was abandoned by Gentiles. His head tilted slightly to one side when he walked, as though his body was at an angle of less than ninety degrees to the street. On weekdays he always had an umbrella hooked over his left arm, never properly rolled, for he never learned how to roll an umbrella. No umbrella on the sabbath, though, when it was forbidden to carry any object. He was not a tall man, and walked with short and rather quick steps. He had remarkably small feet and took a very small size in boots (never shoes). He almost always wore an overcoat, unless there was a real heatwave, with a white silk scarf just

visible under the collar. The walking rabbi was an Edinburgh
institution. Everybody knew who he was. Strangers would
tip their hats to him. Policemen saluted him. Small boys
would tell each other 'Yon's the rabby'. So a street named
after him would seem to be thoroughly appropriate.

Walking was indeed the rabbi's only regular exercise.
He had never indulged in any physical sport in his life.
There had been too much to learn, on both the Jewish and
the western cultural side. Organised rushing about with a
ball seemed to him quite futile. But in walking one could
meditate, or converse with a fellow walker. One could
walk in the King's Park or on Blackford Hill, enjoying
the fresh air. He did make an attempt at golf while on
holiday in Fife, but it was short-lived, and he settled in the
end for an occasional round on the putting green. Chess,
however, was a good Jewish game and he bought a chess
set for his children and encouraged them to play. It could
even be played — according to his ruling at least — on
the sabbath. But the best thing to do when you wanted
relaxation was to 'go for a walk', and he encouraged his
children to do this when they were at a loose end. He
himself was never at a loose end. There was always too
much to do. When the rabbi walked he was most often
walking purposefully to some specific place, if not to the
synagogue to a meeting or a lecture hall or a house of
mourning.

When a Jew died, his or her family 'sat shiva', that is,
observed seven days of mourning during which they were
visited by friends and religious services were conducted in
the home. Of course the rabbi had to visit mourning families.
But there were happier occasions, such as weddings and
barmitzvahs, where the rabbi presided over kosher feasting
and made witty speeches so different from his sabbath or
festival sermons. He was a good after-dinner speaker; for
him this was a happy relaxation and he enjoyed it. Though
he generally walked to such affairs, he could take a tram-car
if it was too far, and of course he went to funerals in one
of the funeral cars provided. One annual event however he

always attended by taxi. This was the inaugural address to the Edinburgh University Jewish Students' Society, which had the rabbi every year to inaugurate their session with a talk and established a tradition that they would always send a taxi for him. One might ask how students, proverbially poor, could afford such a luxury (for it was they who paid). The answer is that there were a large number of South African Jewish medical students, mostly from well-off Jewish families, and they were particularly active in the Jewish Students' Society. There were also American Jewish students studying medicine in Edinburgh because at that time the top medical school in the United States placed severe restrictions on the number of Jews they would accept, and on the rabbi's explaining this to the Edinburgh University authorities many were accepted at Edinburgh. But, in spite of having been discriminated against for being Jews, they were less conscious of their Jewish identity than the South Africans. Anyway, it appeared that South African and American students were not interested in walking, and the former did not deem it proper that the rabbi should arrive on foot to inaugurate a new session of their society. On one occasion the rabbi had completely forgotten that he had promised to give the inaugural address to the University Jewish Society. He heard a taxi stop outside the house one evening as he sat at his desk and immediately exclaimed 'Oh dear, the students!' He realised at once what the taxi was for, and composed his talk as he sat in it on the way to the Old Quad (as the Old College was then called). He was rather proud of this impromptu preparation and of the fact that his speech was as eloquent and as well constructed as ever: it was an anecdote he told more than once.

The streets of Edinburgh the rabbi walked most were in the eastern part of the Old Town and the South Side. When he first came to Edinburgh the old Richmond Street *shul* still existed, and many of the older immigrant Jews lived in Dumbiedykes and St Leonards. Gradually they moved south, first to older streets like Buccleuch Street then, as they or their children improved their economic status, to

Newington and the Grange. So these were the scenes of the rabbi's perambulations. Jews did not live in the New Town, and though this part of the city was product and symbol of the Scottish Enlightenment so dear to the rabbi's heart, it was not, paradoxically, an area he grew to know well. Arthur's Seat and Blackford Hill enclosed the area he knew best. Daiches Braes was on the north-eastern outskirts of the city in an area unfamiliar to him. But Arthur's Seat looked down on it from the south, and its sight would have made him feel at home.

He was at home in Scottish trains too. He was asked frequently to lecture in Glasgow, where there was a large Jewish community, and he knew all the stations on the railway line from Waverley to Queen Street. Dundee too was a city he frequently visited by train; he opened a synagogue there in 1922. His lecturing engagements would take him as far north as Aberdeen and Inverness. He posed as an expert on train times. He always carried in his waistcoat pocket the little paper-bound purple *Murray's Diary and Railway Timetable*, which was issued monthly and gave times of departure and arrival of all trains from and to Edinburgh, with the destinations arranged in alphabetical order. If anyone mentioned going anywhere by train he would pull the *Murray's Diary* out of his pocket and extract all relevant information in a matter of seconds. Occasionally he would travel to London to attend meetings of the English Zionist Federation and other British Jewish organisations in which he was active. (He was instrumental in persuading the English Zionist Federation to change its name to the Zionist Federation of Great Britain and Ireland: he took a strong Scottish position here, and insisted that as a representative from Scotland, and indeed a Vice-President of the organisation, he could not serve if it was merely an *English* body.)

He enjoyed travelling by train, and varying the route by which he came and went. In those days there were two main rail routes to London, by the LNER from Waverley to King's Cross or by LMS from Princes Street station to

Euston. There was also the Midland route, from Waverley to St Pancras, long since abandoned. It was only a few years after the rabbi arrived in Edinburgh that the great amalgamation of railway lines occurred, leaving only the LNER and LMS operating in Scotland, whereas formerly the North British, the Great Northern, the Highland and others operated in picturesque profusion. The rabbi took note of all these things, and felt confident of his mastery of routes and times with *Murray's Diary* safely tucked in his pocket.

It was a train that was responsible for the one physical accident that ever happened to him. He was returning on a dark winter night from lecturing in Glasgow, and found himself in a compartment in a train without a corridor into which an abusively drunk man entered at Falkirk. He decided to get out at the next stop and change compartments. Accordingly, when the train arrived at Polmont he opened the door and descended. However, the train had not quite stopped; the station was unlit; and he stepped from the still moving train on to the dark platform, falling heavily. No bones were broken, but he cut his nose and for a week or so afterwards he wore a piece of sticking plaster across it. He arrived home somewhat shaken, and the following sabbath, for the first and only time until his last fatal illness, did not appear in the synagogue, sending a message by one of his sons to explain about his accident. The scar on his nose never disappeared.

The rabbi bore no grudge against trains or against Scotland for this incident. The drunk man in the train was abusive in a wholly general way. There was no suggestion of anti-semitism in his behaviour. The accident could have happened to anybody. The rabbi was not ever known to express bitter feelings against the drunkard. Of course he disapproved of drunkenness, but it was not a vice with which he normally came in contact. Jews did not get drunk. They drank ceremonial wine on sabbaths and festivals and once a year, at the feast of 'The Rejoicing of the Law', some of them took something stronger. To get drunk (or at least merry) at that feast was regarded by some old-fashioned Jews if not as a *mitzvah*, a commandment, at least as a licensed indulgence. The rabbi however had never observed any of his flock in a state of intoxication: that was a situation quite outside his ken. Not that he would have agreed with the old Yiddish folk-song 'Shikur iz a goy' ('The Gentile is a drunkard'), even less with what the song went on to say ('shikur iz er, trinken muss er, weil er iz a goy': 'he's drunk, he must drink, because he is a Gentile'), a sentiment he would have violently repudiated on two grounds, that it was expressed in the ghetto language of Yiddish, which he had put behind him, and that the sentiment it conveyed was an intolerable affront to civilised thought. No; drunkenness to him was an unpleasant natural phenomenon, and his one encounter with it on the train from Glasgow to Edinburgh was comparable to being blown down in a gale or drenched in a thunder-storm.

The wine that graced the rabbi's table on sabbaths and festivals came from Palestine (then under British mandate) and bore the name of Bozwin ('Beauty of Zion') or Palwin ('Palestine Wine'). It was red and sweet and had no particular character, but it came from the Land of Israel, that other promised land, and it was strictly kosher. For the rabbi such wine was appropriate for Jewish ceremonies. Some orthodox Jews drank only such wine, on the grounds that non-Jewish wine might, as happened in Roman times, have been used in pouring libations to false gods, but spirits came under no such inhibition. It was perfectly proper for the most orthodox Jews to drink non-Jewish whisky or brandy (the rabbi's father in his later years always had a tot of French brandy before dinner, on medical advice, to stimulate his appetite). This might suggest that Jews easily became addicted to the drinking of spirits, but this did not happen.

It was a strange little tale, that story of the drunkard in the railway carriage and the descent from a moving train on to the platform of a dark unlit station. The rabbi used to tell it with a certain dramatic flair, as though it were an adventure he could in retrospect be proud of. And in the telling the drunkard figured as a natural phenomenon rather than as a moral reprobate.

As a part of the Edinburgh Establishment, the rabbi, with his wife, was invited to the royal Garden Party at Holyrood. Afterwards he described to his children how George wore artificial sunburn makeup on his face. This was noted as an interesting fact about the King, not as a criticism. No one could have been a more loyal British subject than the rabbi. Every sabbath he recited (in English: the only English prayer in an otherwise all-Hebrew service) a prayer for the welfare of the Royal Family, asking God, 'who giveth salvation unto kings and dominion unto princes, whose kingdom is an everlasting kingdom', to bless, guard and protect 'our sovereign lord King George, our gracious Queen Mary, Edward Prince of Wales, and all the royal family'. This was very much an Anglo-Jewish prayer, devised in London by the United Synagogue, but the rabbi was happy to use it, in spite of his strong Scottish feeling. There was no question of his praying for any king over the water.

He was, however, a Scottish rabbi, more and more regarded as *the* Scottish rabbi, and his loyalty to Edinburgh was part of a larger feeling for Scotland. He knew the Fife coast from his annual summer holiday there; he knew the cities because of his lecturing there. But what about the Highlands and Islands? He once recited to his children Tchernicowsky's Hebrew version of

My heart's in the Highlands, my heart is not here,

My heart's in the Highlands a-chasing the deer,

and finally, in 1934, decided that the family should take their annual summer holiday in the Highlands instead of in the East Neuk of Fife. So they rented a cottage just north of Kyle of Lochalsh, from where they visited Skye. And the following year they took a small house in Glenuig, almost inaccessible except by boat up Loch Ailort into the Sound of Arisaig and Glenuig Bay or by walking a seven-mile path (there was no road then) from Lochailort station. Here the rabbi would sit by the romantic western shore and watch the sunset; or he would walk up the glen with a book in his hand so that he could sit on the grass or on a rock when he felt tired and read. On the sabbath he would sit by the water and read that day's portion of the Law from his Hebrew Bible and, as the sun set, sing quietly to himself a Hebrew song about Elijah the prophet returning one day to his people, a traditional song to accompany the expiry of the sabbath on Saturday night. For some years henceforth the rabbi and his family were annual visitors to the Highlands. Somehow Highland scenery and Jewish feeling came together in his mind easily and spontaneously. His feeling for Edinburgh derived originally from his student researches into David Hume and the Scottish Enlightenment. For the Highlands he had no such literary preparation. But he did buy a tartan-bound copy of *The Lady of the Lake* on a visit to the Trossachs in 1921 and read it aloud to his children. He liked poetry with a strong and regular metrical beat and firm rhymes.

So the rabbi who was to give his name to Daiches Braes had trodden the Road to the Isles. It is strange perhaps that David Hume and his fellow thinkers of the Scottish Enlightenment had no interest in the Highlands and considered the Gaels to be a wild and primitive people (though one of them, Adam Ferguson, was himself a Gaelic speaker). This view however was modified by Macpherson's *Ossian*, regarded as genuine by some if not all of the Edinburgh literati, who believed it showed the simple nobility of a primitive people. The rabbi probably took an Ossianic view of the Highlanders. His personal experience of them was limited to brief practical conversations with shopkeepers and boatmen, but his European education had left an Ossianic residue. He was rather taken aback to discover in a remote corner of Wester Ross a little Jewish tailor who catered to the needs of the locals and spoke Yiddish and Gaelic with virtually no English. This represented a synthesis he had never bargained for. No solitary Jew living apart from a Jewish community could lead a full Jewish religious life, so this was not really an example of *Torah im derech eretz*. And the repudiated ghetto language preserved in Gaelic-speaking Scotland! He told the story as an amusing oddity.

Of course the rabbi had no difficulty in pronouncing the guttural 'ch' in Scots words, as both Hebrew and German have a similar sound (it occurred in his own name). He laughed good-naturedly at English visitors who talked about 'Lock Lomond'. He was a sort of Scottish nationalist, and used to become really angry when letters to him from abroad arrived addressed to 'Edinburgh, England'. He regarded the English as more provincial-minded than the Scots, and the Jewish community of London as complacently ignorant of the history and structure of the British Isles. In politics he voted Liberal, and would probably have supported a Scottish Home Rule Bill if one had been introduced in his day. At the same time he was optimistic about the British mandate in Palestine, at least in its early years. Later he became more sceptical about the intentions and attitude of the British government. Yet he never wavered in his loyalty to Britain and in the belief that it was the most liberal society then existing. He had no first-hand knowledge of America, though many American Jewish visitors came to his house and he read American Jewish publications. He was amused rather than annoyed by American brashness and was intrigued when he came across examples of American slang. He had a younger brother who had settled in America as a young man and came over once with his American-born wife to visit. It was not a wholly successful visit: the brother, a business man, lived in a different world from that of the rabbi and the brother's wife thought the Scots poor and primitive and their weather atrocious (it rained throughout the visit). But the rabbi would have American students to dinner and show amusement at their accent and at some of their expressions. Once, when there was celery on the table, an American Jewish student declined the offer of some with the remark, 'No thanks; I don't eat flowers.' This was long remembered by the rabbi's family as a striking example of American simplicity.

The rabbi showed no sign of ever wanting to return to the

scenes of his childhood. Yet he was well informed of what was going on in eastern Europe — famine and discrimination if not actual persecution many years before the ultimate evil of Hitler. Year after year he preached from the pulpit about the plight of fellow Jews in those lands and appealed for money to provide relief. Emissaries and representatives from Jewish communities and from rabbinical colleges from Poland, Lithuania and Latvia regularly visited him. At the same time he kept abreast of Jewish affairs in Western Europe and, oddly enough, he developed a special relationship with the Jewish community of Shanghai (flourishing in those days) to whose periodical *Israel's Messenger* he was a frequent contributor. But he himself was happily settled in Scotland and had no desire to travel abroad. His visit to Palestine for the opening of the Hebrew University in Jerusalem in 1925 was a special case, as we have seen. But, even before the shadow of Hitler fell over Europe, he was content to view the Continent from a distance. Once, in the late 1930s, when his elder daughter had graduated in French from Edinburgh University, he spent a holiday in France with his wife, daughters and one of his two sons. Otherwise he spent his holidays in Scotland.

It is a curious fact that his English-born wife, romantic and literary and musical, who shared his feeling for Scotland though more from the point of view of an English discoverer, expected the rabbi, on his return from Jerusalem, to want to settle with his whole family in the developing Land of Israel, and was quite excited at the prospect. She was somewhat taken aback when the rabbi dismissed the whole idea as fantasy: the original Promised Land had its part to play, but his part was to be played in Scotland. The only occasion on which he found himself sharply criticised by Scottish friends was when he innocently suggested that the sparsely populated Highlands could benefit from a large influx of enterprising and well educated Jewish immigrants. Even the most pro-semitic Scot did not want to turn the Highlands into a Jewish settlement. That was not quite what the rabbi had meant, but he never mentioned the subject again.

Although he spoke English with great purity and Addisonian elegance, with no trace of a foreign accent, the rabbi spoke French with a German accent, and over-emphasised the nasal sounds. He knew most European languages, at least to read if not to speak fluently. His German of course was perfect, although he never used it in his Edinburgh years unless speaking to German visitors (and, later, refugees) who had little or no English. There can be no doubt that from the time he settled in Edinburgh in February 1919 he was thinking and dreaming in English. Although he never acquired what could be called a Scots accent, he quickly adopted Scots words and used them unselfconsciously in daily conversation. He once reproved an English visitor for not knowing what an 'ashet' was. He would have been indignant if he had heard one of his English relatives, after seeing the report of the naming of Daiches Braes in the *Jewish Chronicle*, inquire the meaning of 'braes'.

Yes, Daiches Braes commemorated him as a Scottish character, and he would probably be remembered as such long after his rabbinical achievements were forgotten. If at the moment of dying he pronounced the words that linked him to Jewish tradition and history, he would be posthumously Scottish. One lives after death, he once told his children, in the memory of those one has loved and taught. One can also live after death in the name of a street.

CANONGATE CLASSICS

Books listed in alphabetical order by author.

The Bruce John Barbour, edited by AAM Duncan
  ISBN 0 86241 681 7 £9.99
The Land of the Leal James Barke
  ISBN 0 86241 142 4 £7.99
The House with the Green Shutters
  George Douglas Brown
  ISBN 0 86241 549 7 £4.99
The Watcher by the Threshold Shorter Scottish Fiction
  John Buchan
  ISBN 0 86241 682 5 £7.99
Witchwood John Buchan
  ISBN 0 86241 202 1 £4.99
Lying Awake Catherine Carswell
  ISBN 0 86241 683 3 £5.99
Open the Door! Catherine Carswell
  ISBN 0 86241 644 2 £5.99
The Life of Robert Burns Catherine Carswell
  ISBN 0 86241 292 7 £5.99
Two Worlds David Daiches
  ISBN 0 86241 148 3 £5.99
The Complete Brigadier Gerard Arthur Conan Doyle
  ISBN 0 86241 534 9 £5.99
Mr Alfred M.A. George Friel
  ISBN 0 86241 163 7 £4.99
Dance of the Apprentices Edward Gaitens
  ISBN 0 86241 297 8 £5.99
Ringan Gilhaize John Galt
  ISBN 0 86241 552 7 £6.99
The Member and *The Radical* John Galt
  ISBN 0 86241 642 6 £5.99
A Scots Quair: (Sunset Song, Cloud Howe, Grey Granite)
  Lewis Grassic Gibbon
  ISBN 0 86241 532 2 £5.99
Sunset Song Lewis Grassic Gibbon
  ISBN 0 86241 179 3 £4.99
Memoirs of a Highland Lady vols. I&II
  Elizabeth Grant of Rothiemurchus
  ISBN 0 86241 396 6 £7.99
The Highland Lady in Ireland
  Elizabeth Grant of Rothiemurchus
  ISBN 0 86241 361 3 £7.99
Highland River Neil M. Gunn
  ISBN 0 86241 358 3 £5.99
Sun Circle Neil M. Gunn
  ISBN 0 86241 587 X £5.99
The Well at the World's End Neil M. Gunn
  ISBN 0 86241 645 0 £5.99

Gillespie J. MacDougall Hay
  ISBN 0 86241 427 X £6.99
The Private Memoirs and Confessions of a Justified Sinner James Hogg
  ISBN 0 86241 340 0 £3.99
The Three Perils of Man James Hogg
  ISBN 0 86241 646 9 £8.99
Fergus Lamont Robin Jenkins
  ISBN 0 86241 310 9 £6.99
Just Duffy Robin Jenkins
  ISBN 0 86241 551 9 £4.99
The Changeling Robin Jenkins
  ISBN 0 86241 228 5 £4.99
Journey to the Hebrides (A Journey to the Western Isles of
  Scotland, The Journal of a Tour to the Hebrides) Samuel
  Johnson & James Boswell
  ISBN 0 86241 588 8 £5.99
Tunes of Glory James Kennaway
  ISBN 0 86241 223 4 £3.50
A Voyage to Arcturus David Lindsay
  ISBN 0 86241 377 X £4.99
Ane Satyre of the Thrie Estaitis Sir David Lindsay
  ISBN 0 86241 191 2 £4.99
Magnus Merriman Eric Linklater
  ISBN 0 86241 313 3 £4.95
Private Angelo Eric Linklater
  ISBN 0 86241 376 1 £5.95
Scottish Ballads Edited by Emily Lyle
  ISBN 0 86241 477 6 £4.99
Nua-Bhardachd Ghaidhlig/Modern Scottish Gaelic Poems Edited by
  Donald MacAulay
  ISBN 0 86241 494 6 £4.99
The Early Life of James McBey James McBey
  ISBN 0 86241 445 8 £5.99
And the Cock Crew Fionn MacColla
  ISBN 0 86241 536 5 £4.99
The Devil and the Giro: Two Centuries of Scottish Stories
  Edited by Carl MacDougall
  ISBN 0 86241 359 1 £8.99
St Kilda: Island on the Edge of the World
  Charles Maclean
  ISBN 0 86241 388 5 £5.99
Linmill Stories Robert McLellan
  ISBN 0 86241 282 X £4.99
Wild Harbour Ian Macpherson
  ISBN 0 86241 234 X £3.95
A Childhood in Scotland Christian Miller
  ISBN 0 86241 230 7 £4.99
The Blood of the Martyrs Naomi Mitchison
  ISBN 0 86241 192 0 £4.95
The Corn King and the Spring Queen Naomi Mitchison
  ISBN 0 86241 287 0 £6.95

The Gowk Storm Nancy Brysson Morrison
  ISBN 0 86241 222 6 £3.95
An Autobiography Edwin Muir
  ISBN 0 86241 423 7 £5.99
The Wilderness Journeys (The Story of My Boyhood and Youth,
  A Thousand Mile Walk to the Gulf, My First Summer in the
  Sierra, Travels in Alaska, Stickeen) John Muir
  ISBN 0 86241 586 1 £8.99
Imagined Selves: (Imagined Corners, Mrs Ritchie, Mrs Grundy in
  Scotland, Women: An Inquiry, Women in Scotland) Willa Muir
  ISBN 0 86241 605 1 £8.99
Homeward Journey John MacNair Reid
  ISBN 0 86241 178 5 £3.95
A Twelvemonth and a Day Christopher Rush
  ISBN 0 86241 439 3 £4.99
End of an Old Song J. D. Scott
  0 86241 311 7 £4.95
Grampian Quartet: (The Quarry Wood, The Weatherhouse, A Pass
  in the Grampians, The Living Mountain) Nan Shepherd
  ISBN 0 86241 589 6 £8.99
Consider the Lilies Iain Crichton Smith
  ISBN 0 86241 415 6 £4.99
Diaries of a Dying Man William Soutar
  ISBN 0 86241 347 8 £4.99
Listen to the Voice: Selected Stories Iain Crichton Smith
  ISBN 0 86241 434 2 £5.99
Shorter Scottish Fiction Robert Louis Stevenson
  ISBN 0 86241 555 1 £4.99
Tales of Adventure (Black Arrow, Treasure Island, 'The Sire de
  Malétroit's Door' and other stories) Robert Louis Stevenson
  ISBN 0 86241 687 6 £7.99
Tales of the South Seas (Island Landfalls, The Ebb-tide,
  The Wrecker) Robert Louis Stevenson
  ISBN 0 86241 643 4 £7.99
The Scottish Novels: (Kidnapped, Catriona, The Master of
  Ballantrae, Weir of Hermiston) Robert Louis Stevenson
  ISBN 0 86241 533 0 £5.99
The People of the Sea David Thomson
  ISBN 0 86241 550 0 £4.99
City of Dreadful Night James Thomson
  ISBN 0 86241 449 0 £4.99
Three Scottish Poets: MacCaig, Morgan, Lochead
  ISBN 0 86241 400 8 £4.99
Black Lamb and Grey Falcon Rebecca West
  ISBN 0 86241 428 8 £10.99

Most Canongate Classics are available at good bookshops. You can
also order direct from Canongate Books Ltd – by post: 14 High Street,
Edinburgh EH1 1TE, or by telephone: 0131 557 5111. There is no charge
for postage and packing to customers in the United Kingdom.